# IMPRINT
# AFRICA

# IMPRINT AFRICA

## CONVERSATIONS WITH AFRICAN WOMEN PUBLISHERS

Edited by Olayinka Adekola, Jacob Anderson, Joel Cabrita,
Katlo Gasewagae, Bena Habtamu, Brittany Linus, Barry
Migott, Michelle Julia Ng, Anita Too and Kyle Wang

First published 2024 by
Huza Press
PO Box 1610
Kigali
https://huza.press/
E-mail: huzapress@gmail.com

Modjaji Books
https://modjajibooks.co.za/
info@modjajibooks.co.za

Paivapo Publishers
P.O. Box 6120
Rogge Bay
Cape Town 8012
RSA

ISBN 978-1-991240-38-5

Typesetting: Simeon Michael, Brandwiz Business Gengz
Cover design: Megan Ross for Stoep Collective

This collection builds on a class focused on African female authors and publishing in Africa taught at Stanford University between April and July 2020. The editors would like to thank Ellah Wakatama for designing and running a virtual series of editorial and publishing workshops that supported and guided their work on this project.

# CONTENTS

# FOREWORD
## MARGARET BUSBY

The importance of publishing for me is encapsulated in its definition as the activity of making information, literature or other creative content publicly available. It is a no-brainer for me, then, that whoever controls publishing controls the narrative. This encapsulates why it is important for African women to participate fully in the book industry, as a long under-represented group with extraordinary gifts to share.

Add to that the inspiration to be derived from seeing oneself represented, and the outcome is uplifting, even world-changing. Just to know that something is possible makes it worth aspiring to. There is nevertheless the necessity for support mechanisms to deal with any setback that can otherwise be undermining. These things I know from personal experience, more than half a century on from when I became what is invariably summarized as 'the UK's then youngest and first Black woman publisher' in 1967. I never tire of mentioning how I drew encouragement to enter the British literary world from happening upon the work of South African literary pioneer Noni Jabavu, whom I saw featured on the cover of a journal I read as an African teenager at school in 1960s Britain. The publishing work of my countrywoman, Ghanaian writer and cultural icon Efua Sutherland, from the 1970s onwards, would also be a lasting inspiration. Nigerian literary figure Flora Nwapa, the first African woman novelist published in the English language in Britain with her 1966 novel *Efuru* (in the African Writers Series of Heinemann Educational Books), also found time to set up her Tana Press in the 1970s.

So, I was delighted to meet by chance at the London Book Fair in 2018 a young South African publisher called Nkanyezi Tshabalala who testified directly to the ongoing power of the ripple effect, sharing with me her memories of being inspired to enter the profession after discovering while at school various books published by Allison & Busby, the company I co-founded in 1967. Another defining trajectory resulted from first meeting Ellah Wakatama at a 2000 London publishing launch party where we were the only two Black people present, leading to a symbiotic friendship in which there was always a sympathetic ear to discuss how best to negotiate difficulties arising from biased norms within the mainstream.[1] The same would be true of others I met who challenged the status quo, such as Bibi Bakare-Yusuf with Cassava Republic Press and Verna Wilkins, founder of Tamarind Books. Speaking of that process we all went through, of learning as we went along,

---

[1]　Aida Edemariam, 'Margaret Busby: how Britain's first black female publisher revolutionised literature – and never gave up', *The Guardian*, 22 October 2020 https://www.theguardian.com/society/2020/oct/22/margaret-busby-the-uks-first-black-female-publisher-everyone-assumed-i-was-there-to-make-the-tea.

Bibi said in a 2021 interview for *The Los Angeles Review:* 'The internet, Margaret Busby, and many mistakes were my greatest teachers!'[2]  Meanwhile, Verna's passion to see African children part of the publishing process and output found her working with schools in Uganda, involving children there in the editorial process of books where they could see themselves portrayed.[3]

The wise proverb about a stream never rising higher than its source was adapted in 1892 by African-American scholar and activist Anna J Cooper, who elaborated:

> *The atmosphere of homes is no rarer and purer and sweeter than are the mothers in those homes. A race is but a total of families. The nation is the aggregate of its homes. As the whole is sum of all its parts, so the character of the parts will determine the characteristics of the whole.*

We need not reach back to the origins of humans in Africa to recognize why it is vital for women of African heritage to be accorded or, rather, to claim a rightful space in the world of publishing.

The reasoning behind my compiling the anthologies *Daughters of Africa* (1992) and *New Daughters of Africa* (2018) – both commissioned by visionary editor Candida Lacey – included to create inter-generational and international links through which to empower one another, strengthening

---

[2]  Riley Mang, 'Interview with Bibi Bakare-Yusuf', *The Los Angeles Review* (2018) https://losangelesreview.org/interview-with-bibi-bakare-yusuf.

[3]  'An Interview with Verna Wilkins', *Red Earth Education,* 10 May 2016 https://redeartheducation.wordpress.com/2016/05/10/an-interview-with-verna-wilkins/.

the sisterly chain in the process. These anthologies were another form of publishing, each featuring more than 200 women across many centuries, often illustrating the influences that enable our creativity, time and again. It is important also to keep in mind the historical perspective, not only so as not to find oneself reinventing the wheel, but to draw on useful lessons, experiences, possibly to learn shortcuts from those who have already trodden the path.

I was pleased in recent years to share archival insights with Kadija George Sesay as she crowned her publishing journey with a well-deserved doctorate. Remember, too, that there need be no clash between being a writer and being a publisher – something exemplified by sheroes Toni Morrison and Alice Walker, as well as by Kadija and others featured both in *Imprint Africa* and *New Daughters of Africa* (Ellah Wakatama, Zukiswa Wanner, Lola Shoneyin, Goretti Kyomuhendo).

Just as African writers can base themselves anywhere, African publishers should maintain the right to operate from whatever location or locations best achieve their goal. Whether to operate from Kampala or Oxford, Harare or New York, Abuja or London, whether or not to maintain/confine oneself to an online presence – the choices are various and different things are achievable from different bases.

Unsurprisingly, there are notable African women publishers who fall outside the scope of this book – whether Ayebia Clarke, or Irene Staunton of Weaver Press in Zimbabwe. Also, swerving momentarily from the female focus, let us also acknowledge the African men who have taken up the publishing challenge, the likes of veterans Kassahun Checole of Africa World Press or Henry Chakava in Kenya. More recently, Nii Ayikwei Parkes of flipped eye publishing has been spreading the word through publishing as well as writing.

The new can judiciously build on the old, and mentorship is crucial, as each generation inherits benefits from those that have gone before. Iconoclasm is, of course, an option and can give birth to exciting and courageous initiatives, though selective amnesia should be discouraged. (Joel Cabrita's awareness of the danger of erasure is clear from her recent book *Written Out: The Silencing of Regina Gelana Twala*.) For this reason, volumes like this have a critical role to perform in ensuring that the good news – and best practice – is always passed on and remains foundational.

# INTRODUCTION
# JOEL CABRITA

In 2003, the Nigerian publisher Bibi Bakare-Yusuf spoke of a 'rebirth' of Nigerian literary fiction (the occasion was the Lagos launch of Nigerian writer Chimamanda Adichie's novel, *Purple Hibiscus*).[1] And eight years later, in 2011, the Zimbabwean publisher Ellah Wakatama would identify a broader 'African Renaissance' of literature, pointing to a resurgence in populist novels in distinction to the 'high' literary fiction of the 1950s and 1960s.[2] Wakatama and Bakare-Yusuf were only two of many commentators from the early 2000s who lauded the healthy state of commercially viable fiction from the African continent. Members of this new generation of fiction writers were mostly

---

[1] http:// www.cassavarepublic.biz/blogs/main/8319848-the-rebirth-of-publishing-in-nigeria.

[2] Ellah Allfrey, 'All Hail the African Renaissance', *The Telegraph,* 9 September 2011 https://www.telegraph.co.uk/culture/books/bookreviews/8749890/All-Hail-the-African-Renaissance-The-Storymo-ja-Hay-Festival-with-the-British-Council-in-Nairobi.html.

young and many were female (a notable contrast to the male-dominated African literature of the 1960s). Much of this 'new African writing' (as literary scholar Akin Adesokan dubbed the phenomenon) found enthusiastic audiences not only on the African continent but among readers in North America and Europe.[3] Adesokan identified several common features of these works, noting that not only were they mostly written by women, but also that they focused on interior emotionally rich stories and tended to 'end happily, or at any rate, not too grimly'. They were also largely quite short and not overly experimental in literary terms. In short, they offered – and continue to offer – reading material for both African and global audiences that is accessible and popular; they subvert stereotypical tropes about African suffering by supplying more up-beat narratives, often told from a female point of view.

Yet for all this attention on the rise of 'new African writing', the commensurate rise of a new generation of African publishers has been much less commented on. Indeed, many among the aforementioned new African writers have had their work supported by one of these publishers, all of whom have the explicit goal of supporting and promoting fresh African literary talent. Echoing Adesokan, we could loosely call this phenomenon 'new African publishing'. African writers' relationships to these publishers vary widely. Some new writers have first been published by a press in the Global North, and then have had an edition of their book released by an Africa-based publisher. This was the case for Chimamanda Ngozi Adichie's *Purple Hibiscus*, first published by the American Algonquin

---

[3]    Akin Adesokan, 'New African Writing and the Question of Audience', *Research in African Literatures,* 43:3 (2012), 1-20.

Books in 2003 and the first title released by Farafina Books, an imprint of the Nigerian publishing house Kachifo Limited, in 2004. Often the opposite has happened: one or another of the new African publishers have been the first to support authors whose work is later picked up by an international publishing house. For example, Remy Ngamije's *The Eternal Audience of One* was first published by Blackbird Books, South Africa, in 2019, with a North American edition released by Simon & Schuster in 2022.

The new African publisher is more often than not young (under forty or so at the time of founding their press), she identifies as a woman, and many – but not all – of them have transnational existences, living between an African metropolis and a European or North American capital. Some of these publishers base themselves largely or entirely in the Global North but maintain strong ties to the continent. Many come from educated middle-class backgrounds and have professional career trajectories. Almost all the new African publishers have no prior background in publishing nor any formal training in the profession. Many have a strongly felt ideological commitment to promoting African knowledge in a decolonial era, seeing their mandate as undermining the Global North's hegemonic grasp on publishing books about Africa. As part of this broader project of subverting stereotypical representations of the continent, they are interested in supporting new forms of genre fiction typically not associated with African literature, such as science fiction and speculative writing. These new publishers will use digital technology in innovative ways, and they are passionately committed to their publishing houses; many have put their own personal finances on the line for their companies.

The following anthology tells the stories of some of the leading figures within this group. Our goal is to capture a unique moment in African literary history, to preserve a snapshot image of how a small yet influential group of publishers is transforming the African book industry in exciting and provocative ways. What follows is a series of informal conversations with nine different publishers, all either situated on the African continent or located within the African diaspora. Reflecting a key feature of the contemporary publishing landscape, all the featured publishers are women. This is not to negate the fact that much publishing on the continent remains in the hands of men (I am thinking here of the well-established and far more lucrative textbook-educational publishing sector – more on this below). Indeed, many of the publishers featured in this volume testify to the challenges they have encountered as women in a male-dominated publishing industry.

In selecting these nine people, we have applied certain criteria. First, we have aimed for some continental diversity. We have featured two publishers from South Africa (historically one of the strongest publishing centres of the continent): these are Thabiso Mahlape and Colleen Higgs. We have three publishers from East Africa: Zukiswa Wanner based in Kenya, although of Southern African heritage; Goretti Kyomuhendo from Uganda – although Kyomuhendo now identifies primarily as a literary activist not a publisher – and Louise Umutoni from Rwanda. Two of our publishers – Ellah Wakatama and Ainehi Edoro – live in the diaspora (the UK and the US respectively), and a third, Bakare-Yusuf, lives between the UK and Nigeria. In attempting to capture a continental sample of female publishers, we have sought out individuals who operate as independent entities, rather than as part of larger corporate companies. This is in keeping with our broader goal of highlighting the phenomenon of 'new African publishing', an impetus that largely finds its home within the world of independent publishing rather than through multinational publishing conglomerates.

There are many holes in this selection and it is far from a representative sample of publishers across the African continent and its diaspora. We have only featured nine publishers here, and there are – of course – many, many other significant individuals currently active in publishing we could have focused on. We have also skewed towards a mostly younger generation of publishers born between the 1960s and the 1980s. Yet there are pioneering African women publishers who predate this generation, most of all the legendary British Ghanaian publisher, editor and writer Margaret Busby, who was the first Black female publisher in the United Kingdom in the 1960s. Moreover, the group represented here all share a particular legibility for Global North Anglophone audiences; they are linked to the rise of the new African writing in English that has gained a devoted following outside of the continent as well as within. But our focus on these largely Anglophone publishers means that there are certain omissions in our coverage. For example, with exceptions such as Huza Press' Radiobook Rwanda series and Cassava Republic Press' children's books list, for the most part the work of the publishers featured doesn't focus on indigenous African languages. North African, Francophone, and Lusophone publishing are similarly absent from our cross-sample of publishers (although many of the publishers featured here are committed to making work available in translation). Moreover, one of the themes threading through many interviews is how 'African' is to be defined, including whether it is a racially specific term.

Second, while the volume makes the case for a common identity and sense of purpose linking these publishers (many know each other personally, regularly meeting at book festivals, conferences, and launches across the continent as well as abroad), we have nonetheless attempted to represent a variety of perspectives, backgrounds, and professional methods. Most of these individuals have founded their own publishing houses, but not all. One (Kyomuhendo) was an early director of a publishing house, rather than founder. And later in her career, supporting publishing infrastructure has been key to her work with the African Writers Trust. Another (Wakatama) has a long career of working as a commissioning editor for UK publishing houses. Some have entered the publishing world recently (Wanner's Paivapo Books, founded in 2018, is one of the newest publishing houses), while others have been active in this sphere since the 1990s (Kyomuhendo's work with FEMRITE Publications comes to mind). Most publish physical books (Edoro's *Brittle Paper* is the exception), while some make far more extensive use of digital technologies than others (Shoneyin's One Read app is an example of this). Most follow traditional income-generating strategies, but Edoro's online literary magazine is unique amongst the publishers we've surveyed in that it is free at the point of use (*Brittle Paper*'s income is gained via advertising revenue from their website). Some of the interviewees focus exclusively on publishing while other figures also curate festivals, run book prizes, convene writers' workshops, and manage bookstores. All, however, are committed to promoting the work of African writers – whatever this looks like. Moreover, all the featured women straddle the worlds of publishing and authorship in a manner that would be unusual for most publishers in the UK, US or Europe.

In addition to publishing the work of others, our featured publishers also produce their own written work, including novels, poetry and academic scholarship. The overall sense is of a network of intellectuals committed to the promotion and production of the written word in the very broadest sense, rather than a professionalized compartmentalization of 'author' as distinct from 'publisher'.[4]

The genesis of this book lay in a class I taught at Stanford University in April 2020, in the early months of the Covid-19 pandemic. The topic of the class was African female authors and publishing in Africa, a choice that reflected my own long-standing research interests in the history of books on the African continent (at the time I was writing the biography of Regina Gelana Twala, a South African writer who unsuccessfully tried to publish her work, eventually defeated by the gatekeeping mechanisms of a white literary industry).[5] As many within tertiary education found, I discovered that the pandemic brought pedagogical opportunities as well as immense challenges. One such opportunity was the possibility of using the digital platform of Zoom to enable students to engage with publishing figures based on the continent (or in any case, not local to Palo Alto, California, where Stanford University is situated). While it would have been logically near-impossible to bring a group of this size for in-person visits with the class, Zoom meant we were able to speak with six of the publishers featured here during a ten-week class that ran from April to June 2020. I am very grateful to Stanford doctoral

---

[4]  I am grateful to Kate Wallis for pointing this out to me.
[5]  Joel Cabrita, *Written Out: The Silencing of Regina Gelana Twala* (Ohio University Press and Wits University Press, 2023).

student, Chepchirchir Tirop, for her help in organizing these Zoom visits. The last three contributors to the project were interviewed throughout 2021, also over Zoom. The interviews transcribed and presented in this book thus have a discernably oral feel; their genesis was in a series of spoken conversations and our transcriptions have tried to maintain an informal chatty register.

There were nine students in this class and eight stayed on as contributing editors to this book project. One new addition brought the group of contributing editors to nine. These are – in alphabetical order – Olayinka Adekola, Jacob Anderson, Katlo Gasewagae, Bena Habtamu, Brittany Linus, Barry Migott, Michelle Julia Ng and Anita Too. Their full biographies are found in an appendix to this book. Many of these students are either from an African country or have ongoing familial links to the continent (marking them out as a minority at Stanford, where African international students make up less than 5 per cent of Stanford's undergraduate student body). As you will see from their biographies at the end of the volume, many students were drawn to the class because of an already existing interest in African literature and/or gender studies (the class explicitly addressed women's roles in writing and publishing). Not all the students were physically on site at Stanford for the duration of the class. As was the case with our interviewees, some students were residing in an African country during the pandemic. International travel restrictions meant that some were blocked from entering the US; others chose to live closer to their families during this traumatic time.

The members of this class have played a pivotal role in conceptualizing and completing this anthology. They have participated in interviews, they have transcribed these conversations, including following up with interviewees with further questions, and they have offered editorial suggestions as to the parameters and nature of the project. More broadly, the idea of co-editing a book with student participants seemed a faithful reflection of the mood of these conversations. Given that many of the publishers we interviewed spoke critically and at length about the role of intellectual hierarchies and processes of gatekeeping in knowledge production, it seemed fitting that our anthology should seek to muddle traditional hierarchies between professor and students by placing us on an equal footing as editors. That said, in many respects these hierarchies were not muddled at all. Students still had to produce work for the class, which I graded. At the end of the day, I was still their professor. I, moreover, took the lead in organizing interviews as well as in finalizing the anthology for publication, including writing this introduction. Furthermore, student-professor collaborations can mask the true nature of contributions to a joint project, often making it possible for a professor to appropriate the work of their student as their own (this is more common in the sciences, where collaborative projects between faculty and students are the norm rather than the exception, as they are in the humanities). For this reason, an inventory of who performed what labour in the creation of this book is included at the back of the book.

Finally, I am a historian, and the nature of the class students took with me was historical, offering a survey of how writing and publishing on the continent have changed over the last one hundred or so years. Although we spoke with nine contemporary publishers, we were constantly thinking about how to situate these individuals within the longer history of publishing on the African continent. When viewed within the context of this long stretch of time, this group of publishers appears both radically innovative (breaking with publishing tradition in important ways) as well as deeply traditional (cleaving fast to historic trends in the publishing industry in Africa). For this reason, then, I now briefly narrate a history of publishing in Africa. My purpose is not to supply an exhaustive narrative covering the last several hundred years of book production in Africa. Rather, it is to highlight the unique nature of the current-day moment in publishing through contextualizing it within important moments of the twentieth-century story of African publishing.

## PUBLISHING IN AFRICA

Unsurprisingly, the earliest publishing in sub-Saharan Africa was dominated by colonial and missionary presses. Colonial printers across the continent produced official publications including gazettes, decrees and proclamations. More significantly, from the earliest days of missionary activity, multiple printing presses were founded by both Protestant and Catholic missionaries. South Africa's first mission printing press started work in 1861; this was at Lovedale, the Church of Scotland mission station in the Eastern Cape. In Kenya, the first mission press was inaugurated in 1887. Nigeria's first mission press was much earlier, around the middle of the eighteenth century. Reflecting the importance of the biblical 'Word', these mission presses focused on the translation of both the Christian scriptures and their respective hymnals into indigenous languages.[6] From the early twentieth century, mission presses

---

[6]   Charles R. Larsen, *The Ordeal of the African Writer* (Zed Books, 2001), 100ff.

also occasionally published fiction and historical fiction in indigenous languages – sometimes by African authors – viewing the creation of vernacular literature as key to crafting modern 'civilized' Christians.

Mission presses were undoubtedly repressive, reflecting not only the evangelical convictions of their missionary directors but also their racist prejudices about Africans. Certainly, in Southern Africa, African authors had to struggle with censorship from missionary editors if they voiced critical views of colonial rule.[7] Yet at the same time, many mission presses had significant African editorial input, leading some scholars to judge these institutions important crucibles for Black authorship. African Christians also usually steered translation processes, finding in these exercises opportunities to voice their independent aspirations.[8] The influence of mission presses in African publishing persisted well into the twentieth century. In the 1970s, Malawi was exclusively served by five church printing presses.[9]

Most scholars argue that indigenous African publishing only truly emerged in the decade of independence, the 1960s. While this was broadly true, there were nonetheless important exceptions.[10] A small number of African-owned printing presses

---

7   Cabrita, *Written Out,* 122-123.
8   Vukile Khumalo, 'Ekukhanyeni Letter Writers: A Historical Enquiry into Epistolary Networks and Political Imagination in Kwazulu-Natal South Africa.' In *Africa's Hidden Histories: Everyday Literacy and Making the Self,* edited by Karin Barber (Indiana University Press, 2006), 113-142; Hlonipha Mokoena, *Magema Fuze: The Making of a Kholwa Intellectual* (University of KwaZulu-Natal Press, 2011).
9   Oluwasanmi, Edwina, McLean, Eva, Zell, Hans (eds.), *Publishing in Africa in the Seventies* (University of Ife Press, 1975), 217.
10   Oluwasanmi, *Publishing in Africa,* 113.

produced political material across the continent. In Kenya in the decade after World War II, presses operated by Kenyan nationalists emerged, producing handbills, political pamphlets, posters and booklets.[11] In South Africa's Inanda Valley, just north of the coastal city of Durban, a cluster of printing presses emerged in the early twentieth century. Verulam Printers was one of these, owned and run by one D. Motseme. The press published Black-run newspapers such as the radical *Inkundla ya Bantu and Izwi lama Swazi*, the Swati newspaper published by early nationalist, John Nquku.[12] It folded in 1951, underscoring the financial and political difficulties faced by Black presses in Apartheid South Africa.[13] In the same valley, in the Indian area of Phoenix, was also Mahatma Gandhi's printing press. This published Gandhi's anti-colonial newspaper, *Indian Opinion*.[14] It is significant that both these presses published newspapers rather than books. This was a financially driven decision reflecting the lower cost of printing newspapers as compared to books; revenue, moreover, could be gleaned from advertisements. These pragmatic considerations meant that newspapers became influential platforms for literary development across the continent, driving the emergence of new kinds of serialized genres such as the column.[15]

---

[11]  Henry Chakava, *Publishing in Africa: One Man's Perspective* (Bellagio Publishing Network, 1996), 6.

[12]  Eswatini National Archives, Lobamba, File No. 3111, Izwi Lama Swazi, Vol. III, Memo from JJ Nquku, February 5 1947.

[13]  Corinne Sandwidth, 'The Idea of Reading in Early 20th Century South Africa', *Journal of Southern African Studies*, 42, 6 (2016), 1102.

[14]  Isabel Hofmeyr, *Gandhi's Printing Press: Experiments in Slow Reading* (Harvard University Press, 2013).

[15]  Stephanie Newell, *The Power to Name: A History of Anonymity in Colonial West Africa* (Ohio University Press, 2013).

The independence of many African countries in the 1960s catalyzed into being a new kind of publishing. This was the lucrative world of educational textbook production. Newly independent governments identified education as a priority for their nationalist agendas, thereby creating huge new demand for written material such as textbooks.[16] Yet many African governments did not have the immediate capacity – in terms of expertise, staff and facilities – to start publishing at such a great volume. Politicians across the continent solved this problem by creating parastatal publishing firms that partnered with large foreign presses. British educational publishers such as Oxford University Press, Macmillan and Heinemann had existed throughout the continent since the 1950s.[17] Now they received a major boost from newly independent governments, entering into joint ventures whereby they supplied expertise and prefinancing for an easy share of the profits. Tanzania Publishing House, the National Educational Company of Zambia, Uganda Publishing House and Ghana Company were all examples of parastatal publishers partnering with Macmillan in the 1960s.[18] Yet local publishers were almost entirely excluded from this new publishing boom, unable to compete with either the large multinationals or the tight state monopoly over textbook production.[19]

[16] Ruth Makotsi and Lily Nyariki, *Publishing and Book Trade in Africa* (East African Educational Publishers, 1997), 13.
[17] Emma Shercliff, 'African Publishing in the Twenty-First Century', *Wasafiri*, 31, 4 (2016), 10.
[18] M. Suriano, Walter Bgoya, 'Dreams and Constraints of an African Publisher: Walter Bgoya, Tanzania Publishing House, and Mkuki na Nyota, 1972 – 2020', *Africa*, 91 (4), 2021, 578; Oluwasanmi, *Publishing in Africa*, 26, 29.
[19] Oluwasanmi, *Publishing in Africa*, 238.

Local industries were further suppressed in the realm of fiction publishing. Foreign firms would typically extract promising manuscripts from African authors, only to publish them overseas or in Africa through their local branches. Heinemann's African Writers Series was perhaps the most famous example of this. Although the exact nature of the agreements differed from country to country (and some African branches were more autonomous than others), most of the Series' titles were published from London and then distributed across the continent.[20] This was true of a number of other British publishers. As Kenyan publisher Henry Chakava noted, 'Longman and Oxford University Press didn't publish locally, rather their function was to collect good manuscripts and forward them to London for vetting and publishing.'[21] Furthermore, while publishing companies in Europe and North America tended to plough back profit from lucrative textbook publishing into academic and literary books as well as into children's fiction, this was seldom the case with African publishing. Instead of building up other sectors of publishing, British publishers' monopoly over textbooks actively repressed the growth of other literary areas. As Bgoya and Jay note, 'the multinationals that take the lion's share of the textbook market in Africa invest little, if any, of those profits within the country in which they are made.'[22]

[20] Walter Bgoya and Mary Jay, 'Publishing in Africa from Independence to the Present Day', *Research in African Languages,* 44, 2 (2013), 19. See James Currey, *Africa Writes Back: The African Writers Series & The Launch of African Literature* (James Currey: Oxford, 2008), especially pages 1-24.

[21] Bgoya and Jay, 'Publishing in Africa', 19.

[22] Bgoya and Jay, 'Publishing in Africa', 22.

Despite these obstacles, a small but significant number of indigenous publishers did arise throughout the 1970s. Intellectuals across the continent decried the dominance of foreign publishers, perceiving this as out of step with the patriotic fervour of the postcolonial period. A landmark publishing conference was held at the University of Ife, Nigeria, in 1973; delegates declared that 'the time has now arrived for the book industry to become indigenized'.[23] Celebrity African writers such as Chinua Achebe counselled aspiring writers to 'risk their works with African publishers at least once', forgoing 'the jingle of foreign exchange and the glitter of foreign fame'.[24] In keeping with this patriotic mood, many efforts were made by independent publishers to produce texts. Academic publishing was a particular focus, underscoring the belief that knowledge production about Africa should be grounded in the continent. So this was the decade that saw the founding of CODESRIA in 1973, focused on African humanities and social sciences publishing, as well as the formation of university presses such as Ibadan University Press.[25]

Publishers specializing in popular fiction also emerged in these years. The so-called Onitsha market literature in Nigeria was hugely popular with urban readers throughout the 1960s and 1970s. These were thin cheaply produced romance pamphlets printed by small local presses.[26] In 1974, Henry Chakava launched the popular 'Spear' imprint of his own East

---

[23] Oluwasanmi, *Publishing in Africa,* 4.

[24] Oluwasanmi, *Publishing in Africa,* 8, 23.

[25] Makotsi and Nyariki, *Publishing and Book Trade in Africa,* 17.

[26] Stephanie Newell, 'From the Brink of Oblivion: The Anxious Masculinism of Nigerian Market Literatures', *Research in African Literatures,* 27, 3 (1996), 50-67.

African Educational Publishers (the fruit of his successful buyout of Heinemann Kenya[27]), producing short novels for younger readers. Its most popular title – *My Life in Crime* by John Kiriamiti – sold 100,000 copies by 1997.[28] Between 1963 and 1977, about ten other local publishers established themselves in Kenya.[29] The situation in Francophone West Africa was far less vibrant, with the majority of publishing still taking place in France. In the mid-1970s, only about five indigenous publishing houses existed in West Africa.[30] The small number of African independent publishing houses were almost exclusively owned by men. But there were nonetheless important early female figures in publishing. We might here think of Flora Nwapa's Tana Press, founded in Nigeria in 1974, or Asenath Bole Odaga's Lake Publishers and Enterprises Ltd founded in Kenya in 1978. In Ghana, an early female publishing pioneer was Efua Sutherland, who co-founded Afram Publications in 1973 in Accra, Ghana.[31] Of course, in the African diaspora, there was Margaret Busby who as early as 1967 had set up the publishing house Allison & Busby with her business partner, Clive Allison.[32]

These independent publishers of the 1970s faced multiple challenges. New governments gave little support to these

---

[27] I am grateful to Louise Umutoni for pointing this out to me.

[28] Henry Chakava, 'Selling Books in Africa: A Publisher's Reflections', *Logos* 8, 3 (1997), 160.

[29] Chakava, *Publishing in Africa,* 46, 111.

[30] Oluwasanmi, *Publishing in Africa,* 128.

[31] https://www.theguardian.com/society/2020/oct/22/margaret-busby-the-uks-first-black-female-publisher-everyone-assumed-i-was-there-to-make-the-tea.

[32] https://www.asenathboleodaga.com/her-story; https://en.wikipedia.org/wiki/Efua_Sutherland (both accessed April 9, 2024).

publishers, viewing them – at best – as irrelevant players in the provision of educational materials or – at worst – rivals to their own publishing monopoly. Publishers gathered at the University of Ife publishing conference of 1973 listed a litany of the obstacles they faced: 'legislation for authors' and publishers' rights was weak; high government-imposed duties and taxes on book manufacturing materials; insufficient training in publishing and printing profession; inaccessible financing (including high interest on bank loans and overdrafts for publishers); weak book distribution systems across the continent.'[33] Echoing this last complaint, prominent literary scholar, and conference delegate, Abiola Irele noted that 'books published in West Africa are seldom seen in East African bookshops'.[34] Delegates like Irele and others called upon government officials across the continent to ease conditions, to especially relax restrictions on the importation of paper and to reduce import duties on printing equipment and other related supplies.[35]

Political instability also squeezed local publishers. The closure of the border between Kenya and Tanzania in the late 1970s meant that Kenyan publishers lost their export trade not only to Tanzania but also to markets further south. British publishers like Longman and Oxford University Press reduced their presence while most of the indigenous publishers in Kenya folded.[36] The military instability of Nigeria in the 1970s and 1980s likewise meant that many international publishers

---

[33] Bgoya and Jay, *Publishing in Africa,* 19-20.
[34] Abiola Irele, 'The African Publisher' in *Publishing in Nigeria* (Benin: Ethiope Publishing Corporation, 1972), 5-7.
[35] Oluwasanmi, P*ublishing in Africa,* 2.
[36] Chakava, *Publishing in Africa,* 12.

pulled out of the country. In her interview with us, Goretti
Kyomuhendo tells a similar story of how Idi Amin's violent
chaotic reign in Uganda (1971–1979) caused international
publishers to leave the country.

The economic woes of the 1980s only worsened the state of
publishing in Africa. As has been intensively documented by
scholars, serious national crises were provoked by the austerity
measures imposed by international lending banks such as the
IMF and the World Bank. So-called Structural Adjustment
Policies (SAP) led to the collapse of health, education
and transport sectors across the continent. Impoverished
populations lacked purchasing power, meaning books were
more than ever perceived as unaffordable luxuries. Public
libraries also declined.[37] Many of the small independent
publishers of the 1970s completely collapsed during this
decade.[38] Even the larger relatively financially secure parastatal
educational publishers struggled. In compelling African
states to reduce their spending, the SAPs particularly targeted
education. Pressure was shifted onto parents to pay for school
fees and schoolbooks for their children, all of which meant that
declining numbers of textbooks were bought.[39]

Yet by the 1990s things were looking up again for publishers.
Across the continent, new signs of literary life stirred with
independent publishers creating new companies. In 1990,
Walter Bgoya founded Mkuki na Nyota Publishers.[40] Sub-
Saharan Publishers was set up in Ghana in the 1990s and

---

[37]   Suriano, 'Walter Bgoya', 581.
[38]   Chakava, *Publishing in Africa*, 12.
[39]   Makotsi and Nyariki, *Publishing and Book Trade in Africa*, 84.
[40]   Bgoya and Jay, 'Publishing in Africa', 18.

Baobab Press was founded in Zimbabwe in this same decade. For the first time, many of these new publishing firms were founded and directed by women. Sub-Saharan Publishers was founded by Akoss Ofori-Mensah and Baobab Press was co-founded by Irene Staunton (with South African writer Hugh Lewin). There were others too: Longhorn Kenya was created by Janet Njoroge; New Namibia Books by Jane Katjavivi; Focus Publications by Serah Mwangi.[41] All in all, Hans Zell noted in the late 1990s that there were about 300 active indigenous publishing firms in Africa.[42] The 1990s also saw the founding of the Zimbabwe International Book Fair by Trish Mubanga. The Fair became a key annual meeting point for publishers from across the continent, including hosting a conference on 'Gender, Books and Development' in 1999.[43]

This tentative rebirth of the publishing industry was linked to several wider social, economic and political trends at the turn of the last century. For one, many African countries experienced increased political stability during the 1990s. This was a process scholars dubbed the 're-democratization' of the continent, referring to the phenomenon of democratic multi-party elections held across the continent, sometimes after many years of military rule or dictatorial sway. Now a number of multi-term 'life' presidents stepped down in favour of popularly elected officials. New economic flourishing attended greater political openness. The 1990s, furthermore, were a peak decade of international donor aid to the continent, something

---

[41] Mary Jay and Susan Kelly, *Courage and Consequence: Women Publishing in Africa* (African Books Collective, Oxford, 2002).
[42] Larsen, *Ordeal of the African Writer,* 97.
[43] Email exchange with Kate Wallis, April 19, 2023.

that undoubtedly propped up the small flourishing space of
the indigenous publishing industry. Donor agencies saw local
publishing as key to sustaining book supply in Africa and
hence overcoming the disastrous consequences of the SAPs for
education. Gender equity was also a focus for many donors, a
factor that doubtless also encouraged the formation of female-
led publishing firms.

Thus many of the aforementioned new firms of the 1990s and
early 2000s were founded with significant injections of donor
cash. Elieshi Lema, for example, co-founder of the Tanzanian
publishing house E&D Limited – and the only female-owned
Tanzanian publishing house at this time – found resources via
the Dutch embassy's 'Let's Read' books project.[44] The Swedish
Dag Hammarskjold Foundation was a lifesaver for many
independent publishers, who found that banks would often not
lend to publishers (especially female publishers) who were seen
as too risky a prospect. The foundation started a scheme in the
1990s whereby it guaranteed publishers' bank overdrafts.[45] This
is how Serah Mwangi, founder of Focus Publications, was able
to start her company.[46] Okoss Ofori-Mensah received funding
from the Danish government in the form of a private business
loan, on the condition that she had a Danish partner.[47] Bellagio
Publishing Network (an 'informal association of organizations
and individuals committed to strengthening indigenous
publishing in the south') and the African Publishers Network
('a Pan-African network to strengthen indigenous publishing')

---

[44] Jay and Kelly, *Women Publishing in Africa*, 40.
[45] Makotsi and Nyariki, *Publishing and Book Trade in Africa*, 18.
[46] Jay and Kelly, Women *Publishing in Africa*, 82.
[47] Jay and Kelly, Women *Publishing in Africa*, 14.

were similarly funded by donor aid in the 1990s.[48]

The early 2000s continued to be a vibrant time for new publishers with two influential Nigerian publishing houses formed – Kachifo Limited (2004) and Cassava Republic Press (2006). Equally important was the contemporaneous founding of Storymoja Publishers in Kenya (2007). Many of these new companies not only published new writing, but also worked to enhance the overall literary ecosphere by organizing training events for writers and producing literary events. Two such influential literary networks were Chimurenga (2002) and Kwani Trust (2003), emerging in South Africa and Kenya respectively. And although located in a single country, these new organizations had continental reach through their network-building dimension.

For all of this, though, the health of the publishing industry in these more recent years should not be over-exaggerated. While listing 300 active publishers, Zell also noted the 'high mortality rate' of African publishers, and the ease with which a once active firm could slip into oblivion. Extreme financial precarity was the norm of almost all publishers in the 1990s and the early 2000s.[49] Namibian publisher Jane Katjavivi spoke of 'the utter panic of living on the financial edge over a long period of time, risking family and home for the sake of words'.[50] Many of the same problems of the 1970s continued to plague these new publishers, including poor distribution networks, scarce training facilities for local publishers (although new

---

[48] http://www.bellagiopublishingnetwork.com/bellagio_2.htm and https://african-publishers.net/index.php?p=about.
[49] Larsen, *Ordeal of the African Writer,* 98.
[50] Jay and Kelly, *Women Publishing in Africa,* 35.

training centres were founded at Moi University, Kumasi and Wits University in these decades)[51] and a small book-buying public. Trade barriers continued to make intra-African book trade nearly impossible. The continued dominance of Ministry of Education textbook tenders meant that independent publishers still struggled. In 2000, it was estimated that up to 90 per cent of publishing on the continent still took place in the textbook sector; by comparison, the ratio of textbooks to non-textbooks in the Global North in the same year was 60:40.[52]

If we can discern any pattern over the last century or so, it is that the history of publishing in Africa is not a linear one-way trajectory nor a simple upwards curve of increased productivity and success over time. Rather, publishing on the continent – especially small-scale independent publishing – has progressed in fits and starts, highly dependent upon both local economic and political trends as well as international developments. The story of publishing on the continent reveals the continued influence of former colonial powers, especially in the form of British multinational publishing houses and European and US donor governments. The last fifty or so years also highlight the ambivalent role of the postcolonial state, which for many small publishers has not been experienced as a supportive patron but as a rapacious competitor. We now turn to consider the nine publishers featured in this anthology, thinking about how these individuals have managed to navigate these complex dynamics of politics, the post-colony and literary culture.

---

[51]  Jay and Kelly, *Women Publishing in Africa,* xi.
[52]  Bgoya and Jay, 'Publishing in Africa', 22.

## CONTEMPORARY PUBLISHERS

A notable feature of the publishers surveyed in this volume is the fact that all identify as women. As we have seen, this is not an entirely new state of affairs. From the 1990s onwards (and partly driven by donor funding priorities), small numbers of women started founding and directing publishing firms on the continent. Indeed, one of the figures we interview here – Goretti Kyomuhendo – began her career as a publisher in the 1990s, part of this early crop of female publishers (although Kyomuhendo has not directly worked as a publisher for over fifteen years). In the last twenty to thirty years, this trend has become even more pronounced, as evidenced not only by the women we have featured here, but also by other publishers whom we have not been able to include due to space constraints (Akoss Ofori-Mensah, Anwuli Ojoguw, Angela Wachuka and Irene Staunton are a few who come to mind). In addition to building upon a legacy of female-directed publishing firms of the 1990s, the predominance of women in contemporary African publishing may also be due to recent shifts in publishing technology. Ainehi Edoro, founder of online literary magazine *Brittle Paper*, argues that 'there's something about print culture that lends itself to a masculine way of constituting power'. Digital technology, on the other hand, seems to offer more egalitarian and open ways of 'doing' literature, including the ability to work from home thereby juggling childcare responsibilities with professional commitments (Colleen Higgs speaks to this issue in her interview). The internet – and especially digital communications – means that being a publisher can largely take place from within one's own home – a life-changing development for many women with childcaring responsibilities.

One or two of the publishers represented in this volume have a particular focus on women writers (Colleen Higgs, founder of Modjaji Books, for example). However, in comparison to the female publishers of the 1990s, most of the women we have interviewed here do not position themselves as exclusively seeking to publish the work of women writers. We can trace this shift in the career of Goretti Kyomuhendo, previously the first director of FEMRITE which specifically prioritized women writers and now working with African writers of all gender identifications. More than singling out women writers, many of the publishers spoke instead about now intentionally giving space to queer and transgender writers. Ellah Wakatama speaks to this point, also suggestively commenting that Black men may have been left out in the push to include female voices:

> If you are telling the story of our times through
> the point of view that leaves out queer writers and
> leaves out gender-fluid writers of colour or leaves
> out Black men, then our story is not complete.

Where all the publishers agree is on their common commitment to African knowledge production. Again, this is not unprecedented within the history of publishing on the continent. Anger about the Global North's domination of publishing in and of Africa was evident in publishing initiatives from the 1970s onwards. We may think here of the University of Ife's publishing conference of 1973, where delegates denounced the 'cultural imperialism' of foreign publishers, and their efforts to 'subvert the progress of their local counterparts'.[53] We might also think of Margaret Busby in a 1984 *New Statesman* article calling out 'the dominant white (male) community, which

---

[53]  Oluwasanmi, *Publishing in Africa,* 128. decolonize-that/.

controls schools, libraries, bookshops and publishing houses'.[54] This sentiment has only grown over the last fifty years. Indeed, contemporary publishing mirrors the recent interest in 'decolonizing' knowledge in and of Africa, an impulse evident in the number of publications, journals and blogs that take decolonization as their central theme.[55] Much attention has recently been paid to the role of the 'knowledge economy' – including, of course, literature – in reproducing certain stereotypes about Africa. In 2005, Kenyan writer Binyavanga Wainaina's satirical essay published in *Granta* magazine – 'How To Write About Africa' – was a watershed moment, articulating many African intellectuals' anger at the racist writing that Western publications produced about the continent.[56]

Nearly every single publisher we interviewed spoke to this issue. Louise Umutoni, founder of Huza Press, describes her commitment to ensuring that African stories are told from a continental perspective, rather than the African literary canon being shaped by publishers from outside the continent. It is worth noting that all the publishers interviewed here operate with a capacious understanding of 'Africa' and 'African', intentionally including diasporic communities within their definition (this signals a further shift from publishing of the 1990s, which was far more explicitly grounded in the continent alone). Kyomuhendo's African Writers Trust, for example, exists to specifically bridge the gap between diasporic and continental writers. Furthermore, many of the publishers

---

[54] Margaret Busby, 'Black Books', *New Statesman,* April 1984.
[55] As a representative example, see literary scholar Bhakti Shringarpure's *Decolonize That!* book series with OR Books. https://www.orbooks.com/
[56] https://granta.com/how-to-write-about-africa/.

featured here have had personal experience of living in North
America, the UK and Europe – a good number to this present
day. Bibi Bakare-Yusuf of Cassava Republic Press, for example,
divides her time between the UK and Nigeria; Ellah Wakatama
and Ainehi Edoro both live full-time in the UK and the USA,
respectively. But this has not diluted these figures' commitment
to African control of the knowledge production process.
Bakare-Yusuf observes to us that 'publishing is part of the way
in which Europeans have propagated their ideas of superiority
and supremacy'. Equally, however, she argues that control over
publishing signals the dawn of an emancipated new era:

> We can talk about being sovereign nations, yet we
> haven't wrestled with this level of symbolic power
> and the fact that publishing is one of the most
> powerful propaganda machineries going, right?
> And whoever owns that basically captures our
> imagination – and I wanted to.

Thus many of the publishers surveyed here are just as critical of
big international publishers as their predecessors of the 1970s
were. Our interviewees call out these companies for their
entrenched racism, arguing that they continue to perpetuate
certain images of Africa as enmeshed in violence and suffering
('poverty porn') by selecting certain titles to publish over and
over again, rather than giving space to more upbeat forms of
genre fiction (romance, crime, science fiction). Many of the
publishers also identify exploitative financial practices on
the part of these big multinational firms, most especially the
process whereby African publishers frequently struggle to gain
rights to publish African-authored titles on the continent. As
Lola Shoneyin of Ouida Books puts it: 'Nigerian publishers
have to grovel to acquire the rights to publish books that were

authored by Nigerian writers.' And to add to this humiliating experience, publishers such as herself are 'bombarded' with 'ridiculous' reasons for denying these rights, including book piracy (with the implication that such problems don't also confront European and US publishers). Shoneyin describes a situation whereby African readers are compelled to buy Nigerian writers direct from the overseas publisher, yet often they ship books of inferior quality to the continent.

South African publishers are especially critical of these extractive dynamics. South Africa's relatively large white settler community – and the large and powerful historically white publishing companies like Jonathan Ball and NB Publishers – meant that South African publishing followed a unique trajectory compared to the rest of the continent. A South African publisher like Thabiso Mahlape of Blackbird Books is scathing in her view of these large white-owned corporations, referring to them as 'all-white boys' clubs' that shut out newer – especially Black, female-owned – publishers. The large country-wide bookstore chains such as Exclusive Books and CNA (although the latter is in financial duress) are seen by small independent publishers in South Africa as equally problematic. Colleen Higgs labels their 'Sale or Return' policy for small publishers as a 'nightmare' to navigate. Mahlape describes a situation whereby

> I've got about R1.5 million worth of stock sitting
> in the warehouse at the moment. And yet to be
> scrambling month to month to make salaries. Our
> cash is sitting on the floor.

All this has led this group of African publishers to think creatively about publishing networks that seek to bypass, marginalize, or otherwise de-centre the large corporations of the Global North. This might mean identifying new markets outside of Europe and North America. Shoneyin compellingly speaks of a new literary 'Silk Road', describing how she has recently sold the Arabic rights to one of her titles to Rewayat publishers in the United Arab Emirates. Bibi Bakare-Yusuf adopts an opposite approach, but with similar intent. She has recently opened a branch of Cassava Republic Press in London, but with a decolonizing agenda:

> *We're going back to the heart of Empire, to have a*
> *conversation with Empire. Why should it be that*
> *the Empire is always coming to Africa to set up*
> *office?*

As a corollary to de-centring 'empire', all the individuals we interviewed place great emphasis upon intra-Africa trade, circulation, and co-publishing agreements for their titles. This is a much broader phenomenon than merely these nine figures. Publishers Kachifo and Kwani Trust have long worked to transform book launches for new titles into spaces for the formation of 'pan-African literary networks', what literary scholar Kate Wallis dubs 'alternative literary geographies'.[57] A similar impulse is evident among most of our interviewees. Zukiswa Wanner, for example, has worked hard to ensure that African publishers are able to share their titles with readers across the continent. It is for this reason that her publishing house, Paivapo Books, emphasizes translation: 'this is something I've dreamt of for a long time – where we, as an African continent, start to speak to each other across language barriers.' Further

---

[57] Kate Wallis, 'Exchanges in Nairobi and Lagos: Mapping Literary Networks and World Literary Spaces', *Research in African Literatures,* 49, 1 (2018): 163–186.

facilitating this (and reflecting the still-existing infrastructure challenges that make it so hard to achieve continent-wide book distribution), Wanner has recently struck a deal with shipping company, DHL, that allows publishers to ship books around the continent at slightly discounted rates (the scale of the scheme is still quite small, but its intent speaks to an ambitious pan-African vision). But, as Shoneyin points out, by forging creative solutions such as these, publishers are compelled to shoulder burdens one might justly expect the state to carry: 'the truth is that we're constantly having to rebuild infrastructure that's not really our business to build.' Many of the people we interviewed spoke of how publishing in Africa means taking on far more than would be the remit of a publisher in the Global North. Bakare-Yusuf described the multi-tasking challenges of publishing in Africa:

> However, in Nigeria, there's no one path to follow. You have to build your own infrastructure from scratch. You have to be in charge of your own warehouse, selling to the bookshops and even owning your own bookshop. Basically, you're a Tupperware salesperson. You're going around shop to shop selling. In the UK context, most publishers almost find it obscene to touch money. There is a distance between you and money. Money doesn't exchange hands when you're in the UK.

For many of these publishers, a large part of eschewing Western influence is breaking African publishing's historic reliance on donor funding. In part, this is a decision driven by necessity. The UN Millennium Declaration, signed in 2000, identified global development goals including ending poverty and

hunger and establishing gender equality. But they neglected
to include culture and publishing as part of this. The result of
this was that few of the donor initiatives that had subsidized
African publishing in the 1990s survived beyond this decade;
amongst other disappearing initiatives, the early 2000s also saw
the decline of the African Publishers Network and the Bellagio
Publishing Network.[58] (The disappearance of donor aid,
however, was not universal, with Doreen Strauhs characterizing
the most visible 21st century East African writing as emerging
from 'literary NGOs'.)

But many of the publishers also express dissatisfaction with
donor aid on principle, even if in practice they are still reliant
upon outside funding (Bakare-Yusuf has received grants from
Dubai Cares and from the Arts Council, UK, while Huza
Press has received funding from Imbuto Foundation, British
Council, Goethe Institut and Commonwealth Foundation).
Kenyan writer, Yvonne Adhiambo Owuor, recently dubbed
the 'NGO-industrial-complex' as 'guardians of the threshold',
exerting great power over what kind of stories African writers
can tell:

> We could only express our art if we told the
> story that they paid for, one that was about
> how really cool and necessary said NGO was.
> It was the time when stories contained phrases
> like 'empowerment,' 'participatory,' 'girl-child'
> and 'boy-child.' And the NGO world wanted,
> you know, the AIDS, tuberculosis, the weeping
> mother of a dead child, the victim, and, of course,
> the corrupt politician.[59]

[58]  Suriano, 'Walter Bgoya', 586; Bgoya and Jay, 'Publishing in Africa', 23-25.
[59]  https://lareviewofbooks.org/article/decolonizing-history-and-its-tell-
      ing-a-conversation-with-yvonne-adhiambo-owuor/.

Echoing this, Ainehi Edoro expressed to us her sense that 'when you rely solely on external funding, it shifts the kind of work that you do'. So, rather than being subject to donor funding priorities, many of the interviewed publishers seek above all to be self-reliant and financially sustainable businesses. Louise Umutoni described to us how when she was in the early stages of planning Huza Press, she had initially thought her press would be a non-profit. But she soon received emphatic advice from long-standing publisher, Ellah Wakatama, to eschew the NGO funding model.

> I remember Ellah saying to me, 'Well, Louise, listen, you've got to promise me this is not going to be a non-profit. You've got to make sure that it operates like a proper business so you do not do what's been done historically, which is deprive the African book of its value, by not selling it at its value.'

Umutoni goes on to describe how NGO funding 'stifles' the publishing industry by 'distorting the incentive structure around book production and dissemination'. Other figures describe to us their reluctance to be subject to the funding priorities of overseas donors, seeing this as compromising their fundamental commitment to African knowledge production. Along related lines, Ellah Wakatama also pithily denounces the book donation industry (comparing it to the nefarious second-hand clothing industry in Africa), describing how 'free' books sent to the continent from overseas effectively kill off the local book publishing industry.

Yet for all of this, none of the figures we interviewed for this collection are anywhere near financially secure in their businesses. Their dream of financial viability remains just that;

severe financial difficulties are still the reality for all the women we spoke with. Echoing comments of independent publishers from earlier decades, many of the women described how they had put their own personal livelihoods on the line to found and maintain their businesses. These are truly labours of love. Colleen Higgs tells us that she never knows what her monthly salary will be, only paying herself after all the other costs of the business have been dealt with. All have sunk personal finances into their publishing houses, with Shoneyin and others describing how their commitment to publishing African authors has led them into debt, to mortgage their homes, to compromise their retirement funding, and to even worry about surviving month to month. Many resort to working second jobs (sometimes entirely unrelated to publishing) to pay their bills – from Shoneyin's consultancy for a bank in Nigeria to Umutoni working for a micro-grants non-profit in Rwanda to Mahlape using part-time journalism to supplement her monthly income.

Creative use of digital technology is one way in which this new generation of publishers is trying to overcome the perilous costs of the publishing industry. This is seen most prominently in Ainehi Edoro's founding of *Brittle Paper*, an entirely online literary magazine that is one of several similar publications emerging throughout the continent and its diaspora (Troy Onyango's *Lolwe* magazine and Remy Ngamije's *Doek* magazine both come to mind).[60]Edoro speaks in her interview to the relatively minimal costs involved in setting up an online publication like *Brittle Paper* (at least initially). The founding of

---

[60] https://www.nytimes.com/2021/07/17/world/africa/lolwe-doek-afri-ca-literary-magazines.html.

platforms like *Brittle Paper* also underscores how the internet enables African diasporic communities to actively participate in the continental literary scene, further troubling easy distinction between diaspora and continental writers and publishers. The value of online communication is also evident in the many digital initiatives of Shoneyin's Ouida Books, including her launching of a cell phone application, One Read, that offers users a daily story by a different African writer. And during Covid-19 (a challenge that loomed large in our interviews with almost all the publishers), Wanner started an online literary festival, Afrolit san Frontières, with the intention of bringing together writers from across the continent as well as the diaspora. But Wanner nonetheless offers a cautionary note to this tech-utopian narrative, noting how prohibitively expensive internet access still is for many across the continent. Recognizing the challenges of access to the internet, and underscoring radio's status as still the most heavily used electronic media form on the continent, Umutoni's Huza Press prefers to use the 'older' media of radio to promote its authors.

In closing, then, what can we conclude from these varied and wide-ranging conversations about contemporary literary publishing in Africa? As I alluded to earlier, there are many points of continuity with publishing efforts in earlier decades. In many respects, the nine publishers we have spoken with echo publishing concerns that have been articulated over the course of the last century: these publishers continue to reflect upon themes of (post)colonial exploitation of the continent, of economic dependence upon the West and of the need for independence to be realized ever more fully, in multiple registers – including the literary. They express their commitment to 'proliferat[ing] stories by Africans, by Black people', to 'saturat[ing] the world's archives with books written and produced by Black people' (Bibi Bakare-Yusuf, this volume). Yet these dreams are nonetheless articulated in ways that fully reverberate with the concerns and conditions of our twenty-first century globe. The internet looms large in many of their professional trajectories. We see a new awareness of 'Africa' as a global community, as present in London as in Lagos. We hear profound disillusionment with the predatory policies of so-called philanthropists and a heartfelt scepticism about the very notion of 'development'. And turning from the political to the intimate, we can discern in many of the publishers a keen sense of gender and sexuality as fluid constructs rather than fixed binaries. But let us now turn to our nine publishers. It is time to hear their own words about how they continue to find new ways towards the old dream of African-owned literary worlds.

*'I want to be in the business
of making culture.'*

---

## IN CONVERSATION WITH:
## ELLAH WAKATAMA

10 February 2021

**Joel Cabrita:** Could you begin by speaking to your early life and reflecting on some of the influences that you feel have shaped you? Specifically, what resulted in your commitment to African literature?

**Ellah Wakatama:** I was the child who read underneath the covers with the flashlight after lights out. I was also the child who hid up in the tree so my mother couldn't find me and tell me to wash the dishes. It has been my whole entire life, and I think that's a story that many publishers will tell you, that they are readers first and foremost. I think I have one early experience – two early experiences – that have to do with language that are really formative, and as I get older, they get more and more important with time. The first one is that I didn't speak English until I was five years old. I'm the second born in my family and I lived with my grandparents in a village in Zimbabwe from infancy until I was five years old. At that point, my dad was invited onto the Iowa writers' programme. After a year, they decided to bring the whole family to the US, to Iowa. I arrived in Iowa very much a village girl. I didn't know anything and did not speak any English at all. My mother says that I ran to a group of Black children and of course if you're Black, obviously you speak Shona, because Black people speak Shona. I spoke to them and they did not respond to me. She says that for six months I didn't talk, and when I did start speaking, I had a stutter.

My speech therapist subsequently read Narnia books to me. I don't know if any of you have read *The Lion, the Witch and the Wardrobe*? To me, those books were a place of refuge and healing and a place of adventure. The college my father was then studying at was Wheaton College in Illinois and they owned a wardrobe that had belonged to C.S. Lewis. My fourth-grade class was going to visit this wardrobe, so I wore my daisy print raincoat and I had sandwiches, a flashlight and everything, because I was going to Narnia and not coming back. So, of course, when the door didn't open, that was fine too, because there were other kids around and obviously the doors to Narnia couldn't open because the other kids did not know about it. Besides being the trippy kid I was, I think that the experience of reading those books was really fundamental to me, because that series of books did so much for me. It gave me language and also taught me the potential to be elsewhere and to travel through books. So, I think that's my foundation, my origin story.

**Joel Cabrita:** I certainly grew up reading the Narnia books and I saw some of the others in the class nodding as you were talking about them. In your answer you touched on something that we've discussed quite a bit in class, which is the issue of language. I read in an interview you gave elsewhere your account of the trauma of being uprooted and moving to a country where you did not speak the language, and no one understood you. Could you reflect on the significance of language, and especially African languages, for you in your work? Obviously, there's a long-standing debate about what language African writers publish in, whether it's an indigenous vernacular language or English, French or Portuguese.

**Ellah Wakatama:** It's such an important discussion. Ngũgĩ wa Thiong'o, whom I adore, and his son Mukoma wa Ngũgĩ, who is a wonderful scholar himself, speak a lot about writing in your own indigenous languages. Now, my dad was a Shona language novelist early in his life. The preservation of language is really important. Many of you on this call speak another language. There are some things you can say in your mother tongue that don't quite translate to English. I don't know if you have this experience, but I'm a different person in Shona. I'm not quite the same person that I am in English. I think that to preserve all of those emotional states or states of relationship, we do need to preserve language, but only a certain number of people are going to read books published in these mother-tongue languages. But it's still essential to preserve and valorize them.

The English that I speak in Zimbabwe is very different to the English that Bena's family in East Africa will be speaking or Barry or Rachel or Kyle. Not just the accents, but the way that we use the language is informed by that mother tongue. And for me as a publisher, I want to bring that experience of English as 'another language' to my readers. For a long time, Indian writers for example, were considered foreign here in

England. But there was a time maybe twenty to twenty-five years ago when Salman Rushdie and others were writing and Indian English became something that readers all over the world took for granted. We knew what it meant. If I say to you 'Congratulations to Kamala Aunty', whoever has read an Indian novel knows that putting 'aunty' after somebody's name is what you do, right? It becomes familiar. Or if I say to somebody who is West African or has read West African fiction, 'Ehn!' you know exactly what that means.

All of those things start being familiar if we allow the idiom and inflections of those languages in the works that we publish, and so my job as a publisher is to find the best way to do it. To give one example, I do not italicize indigenous languages in any of the books I publish, because those italics tell me that the standard is English and the rest of us are deviating from that. Just as the standard is too often white and male and the rest of us are some kind of deviation. A writer called Nii Ayikwei Parkes taught me this in my publishing of his book, *Tale of the Blue Bird*, because he was insistent that the only things that would be italicized were the things that were being said or thought in English, the rest of it we had to assume was either Twi or Ga, both of which are Ghanaian languages. That's a challenge for the reader, but it's also an assertion that the centre of my world is going to be where I say it is, not where the Western canon has already said it is. And that is the power you have with something as small as whether I use italics or not.

**Joel Cabrita:** I love that example of how the reverse use of italics can effectively decentre English as the normative, universal language. As a personal side note, I had a chapter in a book published recently by Wits University Press, one of the big academic publishers in South Africa, and I made a case of not having italics for isiZulu words, and my request was turned down on the grounds that it didn't meet their style sheet. So what you're doing with your writers is pioneering. For my next question, in thinking about the long sweep of your career and all the changes and developments you've seen as a publisher and editor over the years, can you speak to what you see as the trajectory of African writing, both in fiction and in creative nonfiction? We know there's been a recent resurgence of interest in African writing; what do you see as being the major shifts in the publishing world?

**Ellah Wakatama:** So, the two things that excite me the most are creative nonfiction and genre writing for African writers. People will talk about the grandaddies and some of the grandmothers of African writing, these are people who were writing largely in the 1950s, really important to most of us and their words are still relevant, but their work is very literary fiction. I'm the daughter of someone who was more of a commercial novelist. My dad used to write accessible, commercial novels. Novels with pacy plotting and relatable themes. As a result, I've always been interested in the publishing of commercial literature that has the potential to reach a wide audience. Because for 'literary fiction', only a small number, maybe a tenth of the population, is reading at that level, which is fine because that's how we build cultures, but I also have long wondered about the crime novels you buy in the supermarket. I want to publish Black writers, African writers, writing those crimes set firmly in Nairobi or Johannesburg or Addis Ababa. That change has been coming through only in the past ten years. You see more science fiction, not quite enough romance genre yet, but all those things are bolstering literary fiction writing.

I think that wide range creates volume in the landscape, and the more African writers are writing across the board, the more writers are going to make a living out of their work, which happens most, realistically speaking, in commercial publishing. The international publication of African writers is not because the publishing industry suddenly woke up to talent that has always been there in abundance, it's because of a select number of writers whose work broke out, making money, and so something like *Children of Blood and Bone* by Tomi Adeyemi or *My Sister the Serial Killer* by Oyinkan Braithwaite, if books such as these start making money, then publishers want to replicate that. And so, it's one example of where the commercial impetus is really feeding a diversification of our reading experience in a way I find exciting.

And with creative nonfiction, I've taught courses with a dear friend and writer, Mark Gevisser. About five years ago, we became really concerned with the lack of opportunities for African writers, especially those living on the continent, to get their creative nonfiction published. For a good period of time, I was Deputy Director of *Granta* magazine, and we would commission long-form pieces and pay a substantial fee for the writer to go off, travel, do the research, and so on. That kind of deep investigation, long concentration writing takes money. And very few writers who have to make a living doing other things have that. So we taught a two-week course in Uganda on creative nonfiction. As a reader I am tired of hearing what old white men have to say about the rest of us – I'm directly quoting my nineteen-year-old complaining about her university courses. I thought she put it really well! What would happen if you're writing a story about immigration, for example, and the writer thinks of the continent of Africa as being international but only within the continent, so 'international' doesn't mean London or New York or San Francisco. International means in between Accra and Addis, Harare and Gaborone. What happens there? When you want to write about Ebola, what happens if you ask a Sierra Leonean crime writer who is also a forensic pathologist, to write the piece for you? What do you get that you would not otherwise? This was the approach I took with *Safe House: Explorations in Creative Nonfiction* that resulted from this nonfiction initiative. And that was exciting. I had no particular theme in mind, I just said, 'I like your work, we're going to give you a wad of cash and this much time. Pitch to me, tell me what you want to talk about.' Some of the writers travelled, some wrote quite personal pieces, it was a whole range. Out of that, other initiatives have added to what I think is a really exciting growth in creative nonfiction on the continent generated by writers themselves finding money to put things together. We can all only benefit from that.

**Brittany Linus:** I'm curious to hear your thoughts on the Afro-fantastical and Afrofuturism as a genre. Have you seen any fiction works written in that vein? What sort of impact will Afro-fantastical work or Afrofuturism have on the continent?

**Ellah Wakatama:** I often have trouble with definitions, especially with the whole Afrofuturism thing. I know it when I see it, but it's hard for me to define. I am a fan of speculative fiction; I always have been. I haven't always been able to work on it because I'm primarily a literary fiction and nonfiction publisher. One of my jobs right now is commissioning an original fiction full-length book for Audible. When they asked me, I said I would do it if I could do genre. Science fiction is something that I'm doing and I'm also making sure that I am commissioning African writers to write science fiction. I have one non-binary writer based in the west coast of the UK of Nigerian origin. I have a white South African writer writing science fiction for me. I have a Brazilian-American Black writer writing another science fiction novel. So in the next couple of years, my hope is that my list of Afro-speculative fiction will come alive. If you look at short stories, there's a lot of amazing stuff right now. Also, think of the wealth of untapped material we have. Think about Yoruba culture or Voodoo in Haiti or Candomblé in Brazil, and all the other African religions that haven't yet been written into speculative fiction, let alone concerns of language and folklore and the primordial soup of speculative fiction. Science fiction and any sort of futurism are really good ways to find innovative ways to think about the now. I don't know if you've come across Tade Thompson? He's one of my favourite science fiction writers. Mighty, mighty guy. He wrote the *Rosewater Trilogy*.

**Joel Cabrita:** On this topic of expanding the genres of African writing, and this greater interest in commercial popular literature, we've also looked at the Pacesetters novels of the 1970s in our class. It was great to hear from Barry Migott and Anita Too about their perspective of the novels. Both of them grew up in Kenya and grew up reading these novels for fun. We thought about how this really significant genre – in terms of the number of people reading these paperbacks – goes under the radar, not classed as 'respectable' literature despite being so influential.

**Ellah Wakatama:** Yeah, and it's almost like a gateway drug. You start there and next thing you know... [laughter]

**Joel Cabrita:** As you know, this class focuses not only on African writers and the publishing industry in Africa, but also specifically on writers who identify as women. In your comments about the influential generation of writers from the 1950s, you referred to the grandaddies and the very few grandmothers of African literature. Can you speak to gender in African fiction and nonfiction at the current moment?

**Ellah Wakatama:** If you consider the obstacles that women and African women have faced in terms of writing a novel and then think that we can still name Bessie Head, we can name Doris Lessing, we can name Mariama Ba. The fact that I can come up with these names that just roll off my tongue is evidence of the massive willpower of these women. And then it also makes you think about those women writers who never quite made it to that point. For example, Tsitsi Dangarembga, who is still alive now. She was the first Zimbabwean woman to have a novel published, and she's now only in her late fifties or sixties. That's pretty astonishing. I don't necessarily think it was about keeping them out, but access was a problem. And it always has been. Even when I started working, it was a problem for African writers and African women. The question is, where do I send my book? I don't know any editors or publishers. How does this even work? For a long time, even now, it's been made so difficult to reach that point. If you're the first person in your family to be able to read and write, or the first person to have an education beyond primary school, then where are you going to make those contacts? Breaking down those barriers to access has allowed us to take advantage of the real talent that is available. It's all about volume, really. The numbers of African women writing has grown dramatically.

I am now becoming concerned about the state of access to publishing for men of colour and for queer writers of colour. We could all name ten African women writers, starting with Chimamanda Ngozi Adichie. There are just so many African women – I think of Maaza Mengiste – who are selling on an international level. It is much harder to find the same volume with Black male writers or queer writers. It is something that is starting to be addressed, but for me it's an important area of focus. I reckon that if you are telling the story of our times through the point of view that leaves out queer writers and leaves out gender-fluid writers of colour or leaves out Black men, then our story is not complete. I think that these things are – and I don't want to sound glib – easy to fix. You know what's lacking on the bookshelf. At least for me as a publisher, if I think there's something lacking, then it is my job to fix that. It is about knowing that you, as an acquiring commissioning editor, have the power to say, 'This is what I am looking for', and 'Let me help you amplify your voice'.

**Olayinka Adekola:** You've described how there's a lack of queer African voices in the literature sphere. I also know that often homosexuality and queerness are very taboo. How can you work around that as a publisher to produce this work that needs to be heard? Also, how is it received?

**Ellah Wakatama:** Fab question, huge question. There is a lot more writing from queer writers and gender fluid writers and trans writers because we are in an era where people are defining themselves and demanding to be called by their names. And not just in Western countries. I think that one of the great misconceptions is that all Africans are homophobic, and all Africans deny any kind of non-binary gender identity. If you look at traditional African societies, every single one has a way of accommodating those of us who are different in that respect. Yet, mostly because of religion, both Christianity and Islam, we have leaned towards a fundamentalism that is very much based on a Western conception of gender binaries. So our ways of living as people are now forgotten. A lot of writers who I work with are wanting to give voice to the fact that certain sexual identities are not Western but can be deeply rooted in African culture. I'll mention Akwaeke Emezi, for example, who is non-binary and writes very much from their own traditional cosmologies, both as a Sri Lankan and a Nigerian.

And there is the very real fact of danger for people, either publishing or writing about these issues around sexuality and identity. In some countries you can get killed. One, as a publisher, has to be very sensitive to the fact that it may just be controversial in a Western country but in another country, it is a matter of life and death. Care for your writers is really important and you have to be sensitive. At the same time, people within those countries are fighting those fights themselves. It's not as if activists are waiting for a Western publisher who swoops in to save the day. I have publishing friends in Uganda, in South Africa, in Kenya, who are all working to fight those battles. What's exciting is that these developments make for a whole genre that is melding an understanding of who we are as people with issues around human rights. It can make for really beautiful fiction, great poetry, and life-changing creative nonfiction.

**Joel Cabrita:** You were awarded an OBE in 2011 – that means Officer of the Order of the British Empire, an award given in the UK for exceptional service in the field belonging to the awarded individual. Many in this class won't be familiar with the British honours system, but they might find it startling to hear the words 'British Empire' used today, especially in the context of Anglophone African writing. Can you speak to how you've made sense of that award, given the work that you do?

**Ellah Wakatama:** No one has ever asked me that! I've had an answer ready for ages and nobody has ever asked me! Why is an African – and a rather emphatic African – accepting an award from the British Empire? When I got the note from [Buckingham] Palace, I phoned my mother and said, 'This is problematic.' And she said, 'They invited you to their chief's village to be honoured by the chief. You go to the chief's village and take that honour because we have worked hard for it.' And I think she was absolutely right. (Just a caveat, I could just be justifying this because it was great to go to the palace!) But I can choose to define what the honour means. The honour opens doors that allow me to say things and be taken more seriously in some cases. It's also an award that comes as a result of my peers recommending me and lobbying for me to get it. You don't apply for it. For me, that was very moving, that people who I hold in great esteem were recognizing the work that I was doing. And the award came at a moment when I felt I was fighting all the time for my writers, fighting to change things. So when it came, it felt as if I wasn't as invisible as I thought I was. That was really important. But back to my mother, the chief invited me to the village to give me an award and so I went. I even curtsied!

**Joel Cabrita:** Your answer reminds me of what you were saying a moment ago about refusing to accept that English is not an African language. Are you suggesting that the British Empire and colonial experience can also somehow be Africanized?

**Ellah Wakatama:** I don't know if I would be as categorical as that. We cannot forget that settlement and colonization were repressive, that it was a system based on the rape and pillage of our countries and our resources. My job is about definitions and a lot of it is about saying, 'You may think this is what it means, but let me tell you what it means for me.' That shifts the centre. I keep repeating it but for me it's really important, it's entirely possible. At college in Indiana at the age of nineteen, an African-American student asked me what it was like to grow up as a minority in Rhodesia, now Zimbabwe. I didn't know what she meant. I wasn't a minority, everybody was Black. My best friend was a white Zimbabwean who was freaked out when first coming to England because everybody was white. She wasn't used to seeing herself mirrored in that way. I think what I understood much later was that for my fellow student 'minority' meant a person of colour, regardless of where you were in the world, right? You can either allow that to be your identity, or you can say, 'Wait a minute, there are actually more of us Brown and Black people in the world. We're actually the majority.' That shifts the centre. Make that definition your definition and move forward.

**Kyle Wang:** You've sat on the judging panel for the Man Booker Prize and of course you're now currently the Chair of the Caine Prize for African Writing. What has been your experience sitting on book prize panels and having all of these judges with different reading styles come together to make an artistic decision?

**Ellah Wakatama:** I love your question, Kyle, thank you. So, as the Caine Prize chair, my job is not very glamorous. I have to run the prize in terms of strategy and finances and so on. But what's really exciting is that I also get to lead in choosing the judges each year. What you pinpointed there – the different reading styles on a panel – is really important. I want to get a whole range of those. I make it a point to choose one judge who is not a writer. Most recently, that judge was a choreographer. It's also important for me to have judges based in different African countries and reflecting very different styles of approaching literature. Out of that kind of diversity, you get excellence because they are all coming at it from different perspectives, arguing with and persuading each other.

When I judged the Man Booker Prize, I was the first African judge they had ever had and that was 2015. That's really horrifying. Since then, there have been several, including my friend, Margaret Busby, chairing the prize last year. I was delighted to be asked. That meant that I was injecting a different kind of reading into that panel. I love judging panels. One, because I like being in charge and saying what's good [laughs]. Two, because I love giving money away to writers. Three, because you learn so much from how other people read. I know the European canon, I know American literature, but I also know African literature and I have an interest in Asian literature. So my reading is very much from the point of view of someone who wants to read the whole world whereas another reader might be quite specialized and have a particular interest. We're all going to bring different things to that judging panel, and if we are cordial then you get a better result. You can shift the way that a prize goes by your choice of judges. It's so important.

**Katlo Gasewagae:** Ellah, I have two questions for you. One is also about the Caine Prize. One of the questions we've pondered in class is the work that institutions like the Caine Prize and other gatekeeping institutions can do to transform literature coming out of Africa, reaching beyond just stereotypical depictions. My second question is around the term 'African literature'. Is there a conversation in your circles around expanding our definition of African literature, expanding the genres that are awarded prizes like these, or awarding more than one story for a number of different genres, rather than just calling it all 'African literature'? It seems to me that choosing a single work across fifty-plus countries, writers from which are exploring many different themes in many different ways, fails to recognize the diversity in story and genre that is contained within the work coming out of the continent.

**Ellah Wakatama:** I'm going to answer this one about definitions first. This is a conversation that comes up every single year. What is an African writer? I hate saying 'African writer' because what does that even mean? My definition that I use for the Caine Prize – because you have to have some rules – is that it's somebody who has an African parent (one of their parents has an African passport) or they themselves are a citizen of an African country or they have an African passport. Every year there are arguments about that, but until somebody can come up with a better way for me to define it, that's what I'm going to go with. You are right that it is a challenge to decide on one best story from so many different countries, but I would challenge you to come up with a better way for us to do it.

What you see is that over time there are trends in the things that authors are writing about. That can be troubling. People are very much against 'poverty porn', but I don't know if you guys have come across NoViolet Bulawayo, the Zimbabwean author of *We Need New Names*. She was accused of that by someone who is also a dear friend and someone I admire, but who in a review called NoViolet's work poverty porn (I don't know if those were his exact words). NoViolet responded that that is how she grew up. They were that poor, and that she couldn't be told she was reiterating a stereotype if she's telling you what her real life was. So we can acknowledge the huge multiplicity of experiences of Africans and to say that within those experiences, what we're looking for is excellence. And that excellence can encompass so many different things.

Going back to Kyle's question, the only way that you as an institution can influence the literary landscape is to make sure that you are careful enough about choosing judges and sourcing where those stories are going to come from. So are you speaking to that new literary magazine from Eswatini or from Nairobi? Have you contacted them to say, 'Send us your stories'? If you do that really hard groundwork, then your judges are free to concentrate on excellence across the board. I think we do a pretty good job, especially in the recent past, in the kinds of stories that make it to the Caine Prize. I agree with you; it's a frustration, but you have to have some kind of mechanism for doing this. And don't forget that the end result is that we give a wad of cash to a writer, hopefully changing their lives.

**Rachel Clinton:** I actually had a similar Question to Katlo's. A lot of African stories that are told are from Nigeria, Kenya and South Africa. There are a lot of other countries that go 'undiscovered' in the literary world. What are your thoughts about this? How can we promote authors to submit stories from countries that aren't in the limelight as much?

**Ellah Wakatama:** We go back to that centring conversation. These writers may be undiscovered by Western writers, but Africans are reading each other. Listen, there are more Nigerians than the rest of us and they are a mighty people. I just surrender to it [laughs]. Also, I love Nigeria, particularly Lagos. But there are more Nigerian writers by sheer force of numbers. Kenya also has a really vibrant literary life. Mostly because of the energy of Kwani and other initiatives – the work that Kwani did purposefully to spearhead the development of Kenyan literature, Kenyan fiction, and nonfiction.[1] That's really important. The same thing is now happening in Uganda. I know you're also speaking with Louise Umutoni from Rwanda. South Africa has such a strong publishing industry that is now including its wider population, not just its white population. And there are reasons for all of those spaces being more 'seen' on a more international basis.

I do think, Rachel, that you would find the work being done internationally to amplify the voices of writers from other countries or writing, for example, in French and Portuguese, is really encouraging. I do a lot of teaching of editors and publishers in African countries because I want part of that

---

[1]  Akin Adesokan, 'New African Writing and the Question of Audience', *Research in African Literatures,* 43, 3 (2012), 1–20.

conversation to remain on the continent. We don't always need to be talking to people in London and elsewhere, we can just talk to ourselves and that is really important as well. But you want your writers to make money – I want my writers to make money – and there is only a certain amount you're going to make only publishing in Harare, for example. You'll make more publishing internationally. But in terms of intellectual input and culture, those conversations we have with each other are vital and actually more important in terms of defining ourselves. It's something that Indian and Asian writers have done very well and that I think we are starting to do better for ourselves as African writers and publishers.

**Joel Cabrita:** In Louise Umutoni's conversation with us (see page 133 in this volume), she recounted a conversation that she had with you when she was starting up Huza Press and it was about whether it would become a publishing company that relied on NGO funding or not. You were very adamant that this had to be a commercially viable press, that it shouldn't be indebted to 'philanthropic' funding, and it had to make sense in terms of money.

**Ellah Wakatama:** I believe that so emphatically. I'm really against book donations to African countries. I don't know if any of you who have family in African countries know about those big markets where they're selling clothes from the United States, which actually kills the local textile industry. The same thing happens with publishing. If you are waiting to have books donated to you, who has written those books? Where are they coming from? You're killing your own local industry. The emphasis should be on building that local industry so local writers have somewhere to go rather than importing those books.

**Michelle Julia Ng:** I am not from Africa; my parents are not from Africa; I'm not African. But I'm inspired by this topic. Apart from not donating books, what's the best way to help for outsiders like myself to be active supporters of African literature?

**Ellah Wakatama:** I reckon that you should buy the books, Michelle. If you're interested in a certain part of the world, buy the books, and hear what the people have to say. You often hear somebody saying rather grandly, 'I'm giving a voice to the voiceless,' which is actually crap because nobody's voiceless. I'm not voiceless if you choose to hear me. And vice versa. It's about reading the work and that is the biggest form of support you can give. Also, always insisting in whatever environment you're in, on that range and finding ways not to say 'diversity', because I think that it's another one of those words that has fast become meaningless. It's almost the same thing as 'ethnic' and basically means Black and Brown people and not white people. That's not helpful because that's not centring ourselves. I think it's about actively saying in the space, 'I can't participate in this intellectual exercise because the premise is flawed,' and what can you do about it.

At my liberal arts college, I was a communications major, but I had to take English classes. I looked at the [reading] list and I said to the professor, 'I'm not reading these books because it's too many dead white male authors.' I was quite a good student, so the professor said I could come up with my own reading list as long as it was comprehensive and I did all of the work. So I spent a whole year only reading Black women, and that was so good for me. It's having the courage and perhaps the youthful arrogance to say, 'I can't participate in this exercise because the premise is flawed. And the flaw is that you have not included this, this, and this, can we please explore that'. Because you have power, as a student, you are paying salaries. As a consumer, you are paying for my industry. Therefore, make those demands.

**Katlo Gasewagae:** My final question is about the commercial impetus. We've seen the commercial impetus be detrimental, for example, in pigeonholing work that gets awarded international book prizes. Talk to us about the tension that exists around publishing work that sells versus work that matters.

**Ellah Wakatama:** Woah, lady! Okay, that's good, a very difficult question. For me, publishing is primarily about building culture. What I want to do is establish that bookshelf that my grandchildren will refer to. And the shape of that bookshelf is really important to me. So that is a lifelong project. Those have to be books that sell because otherwise the writer can't afford to continue writing. I can't afford to continue being a publisher. That's where the commercial impetus is. But if you get the balance right, you have a publishing house that, for example, has writers who are selling at a commercial level, but also writers where you take a punt and think, maybe 'nobody' (or around 5,000 people) will buy this book. But it could be 5,000 people this year and the book will continue to sell. I don't think there is a single book I've published that doesn't matter. It's important to know that a science fiction or a romance novel, if it's written from a certain perspective, it too is political, urgent, and can make a massive difference. Those books can also sell, but it's a constant tension. And you just have to make decisions for yourself as a person. Do I want to live my life publishing books that don't matter but sell? No, because that's a waste of a life. If I want to be in the business of making culture and the books have to matter, the money is still vital because the writers have to eat. As do I!

**About Ellah Wakatama:** Ellah is an editor-at-large at Canongate Books. She is Chair of the Caine Prize for African Writing and served as a judge for the Man Booker Prize in 2015. She was founding Publishing Director of The Indigo Press, Series Editor of the Kwani? Manuscript Project and has edited the anthologies *Africa39* (Bloomsbury, 2014) and *Safe House: Explorations in Creative Nonfiction* (2016). In 2011, Ellah was awarded an OBE for service to the publishing industry and in 2018 she was made an honorary fellow of the Royal Society of Literature.

*'Let's proliferate stories by Africans,
by Black people. Let's saturate the world's
archives with those kinds of books.'*

## IN CONVERSATION WITH:
## BIBI BAKARE-YUSUF

17 February 2021

**Joel Cabrita:** Bibi, thanks so much for being here. To begin the conversation, would you mind telling us about some of the influences that have shaped you?

**Bibi Bakare-Yusuf:** I would say the Yoruba women who surrounded me were probably my earliest influence. These were very economically powerful, unlettered women who ran the show. They made me feel that the world belonged to me, and I could aspire to whatever it was that I wanted to be.

I had a mother who was truly inspirational because she had a strong sense of the archive. This sense of the archive has always been with me. We would travel to Europe every summer and my mother would always want us to take pictures at all the monuments. I would get very irritated at having my pictures taken, and she would say, 'You know, you have to take pictures so that no one can ever tell you that you never went there. You went there, and you saw.' To my ten-year-old ears, who cared whether I went to a place or not?

I didn't fully comprehend the significance of her words until years later when I was studying anthropology, where I was encountering all the racist literature and the idea that Africans were lesser people, inferior to Europeans. Suddenly the truth of my mother's words – 'you were there, no one can ever say to you that you never came to a place' – had never been more true, more significant for me. So those women were my formative inspiration, before literature, before text.

Text came much later for me. I read a lot but I think it was the stories around me that were most influential. Of course, I could name writers, but I think what I really want to leave you with, in terms of my own inspirations, was the indomitable spirit of the women around me, and the ways in which they dealt with issues around patriarchy, issues around their own sense of self, the importance of women owning and having financial wealth. If you can have your own money, everything else becomes possible. You can have your sense of agency in the world. So, of course, when I went to do my PhD, it's no coincidence that it was about women's embodiment and agency.

**Joel Cabrita:** That's very powerful. We know you founded Cassava Republic in 2006. I know from reading existing interviews with you that you had no prior background in publishing. So founding a publishing house seems like such a brave and ambitious thing to do. We'd love to hear more about it, including some of the main challenges you've faced along the way.

**Bibi Bakare-Yusuf:** I think it takes a certain kind of madness to start a publishing company. The reason why I say it takes a certain insanity is because the history of publishing is wrapped up with power, with imperialism, with the 'civilizing mission'. Publishing is part of the way in which Europeans have propagated their ideas of superiority and supremacy, using the written text. Think of the ways in which the Bible was initially taken away from the powerful and was democratized. Being once a tool of liberation, the Bible also became the very instrument by which Black people and Africans were subjugated, and [by using it] Europeans could spread their wings and their own sense of power in the world. So, I think with that kind of history, [starting your own publishing company] has to take a certain insanity. That's number one. And number two, publishing arose out of a certain elite gentlemen's club where they wrote and shared their texts amongst themselves.

So why would I decide to start a publishing company? It was very simple. I arrived in Nigeria to take up an academic position, as a visiting scholar at a university and I was appalled by the kinds of books I saw on people's bookshelves as well as in the bookshops. People were talking about *Chicken Food for the Soul* and what's his name? – John Grisham. You might think this is a certain snobbery on my part. But I found the idea of being a right-thinking person [yet] the only books you'd have on your shelves would be a diet of John Grisham, Danielle Steel, the Bible, *Rich Dad, Poor Dad,* troubling. I thought to myself, we simply cannot build institutions or build a civilization on this kind of meagre diet. It's just too dangerous that we have to consume so much of the West. Here is a continent of stories and yet people are not consuming them. So I thought, somebody should start a publishing company that's going to provide a platform for writers to tell their own stories.

I thought that it's not enough for Africans to be telling their own stories. Black people, wherever we may be, have to own the means of production and owning the means of production is the missing link from my perspective. Africans have been writing stories for millennia but the machinery for the dissemination of these stories in the modern world has not been ours. That was one of the things that motivated me: that we have to own the means of production. We simply cannot allow for our instrument of ideas, of our knowledge production, to be owned solely or entirely by Europeans and Americans. We can talk about being sovereign nations, yet we haven't wrestled with this level of symbolic power and the fact that publishing is one of the most powerful propaganda machineries going, right? And whoever owns that basically captures our imagination – and I wanted to. Arrogant as that may sound.

You have to understand the context in which Cassava Republic was established. It could never ever have been established in the UK because you're in an environment where you do not see examples of Black people doing that kind of stuff. There were no role models for you to emulate so that you can even begin to imagine the possibility that you can do something like publishing. Then I find myself back in Nigeria where you meet people, and everyone's on to something, everyone's about to invent something and about to do something. You're in that environment where you think, 'Okay. I want to do this. I can make this manifest. Go online, find out how you do it.'

The ways in which publishing is done in the UK, in America, do not necessarily work in this environment. In America, in the UK, as a publisher you acquire books primarily through an agent, you pay the advance and then you edit the book, and from the moment you print the book, the books go straight to the distribution house and another company takes care of it. As a publisher, printing a thousand, two thousand copies, you never physically see two thousand copies. Somebody else takes care of that. And another company takes care of going to bookshops and selling to them. All of these templates were already there for me to emulate upon setting up in the UK.

However, in Nigeria, there's no one path to follow. You have to build your own infrastructure from scratch. You have to be in charge of your own warehouse, selling to the bookshops and even owning your own bookshop. Basically, you're a Tupperware salesperson. You're going around shop to shop selling. In the UK context, most publishers almost find it obscene to touch money. There is a distance between you and money. Money doesn't exchange hands when you're in the UK. It is similar to the way all of us are abstracted from the things we consume. Rather than saying we're eating pig, we say we eat pork so we don't have to deal with the reality of the sentient being that we're consuming. We have these fanciful names for all the things that we do.

So for us here, we have to deal with the challenges of having your own warehouse and the cost of that. Having to go to the bookshops and trying to sell to them directly when in other markets that would not be the case. You sell the books to them and even after selling the books, there's no guarantee that you'll get paid. And that begins another round of chasing for money and creating distrust with authors. So, it was a real baptism of fire for me, so to speak.

And then there's the problems of printing books. Because of the low printing quality in Nigeria at the time, we were forced to print abroad and with printing abroad comes the issue of how to deal with ports and logistics. I know much more about Nigerian maritime law than I should. I really don't care about

it, but I have that information in my head. A British publisher
in the UK doesn't have to think about that. Things are a lot
smoother for them. It's that kind of physical material challenge
at a structural level that we have to deal with in the Nigerian,
African context. And there's also a symbolic challenge at another
level – there's a tacit lack of belief amongst our own because
we have been so trained into ascribing knowledge production
and efficiency to whiteness. So, we can consume knowledge,
but its production is made possible by white people. It makes it
difficult to gain trust among authors and amongst journalists.
These are real challenges that we often don't talk about. People
don't trust that these books were produced by mostly Black
people. Cassava Republic was started by myself and my ex-
husband, who is white. Even though this was my idea, and he
was not involved in the day-to-day process of the company – he
was a financial contributor, as I was – for a lot of people, the
assumption was always that he was the brains behind Cassava
Republic, and I'm just a figurehead for it. That has to do with a
certain anti-Blackness that we also have within ourselves and
this is a real challenge that we don't talk about.

But I would be remiss if I only talk about the challenges.
Challenges also provide opportunities – opportunities to do
things differently and to have direct relationships with our
consumers. In the UK, because publishing is mostly mediated
through middle people, you don't have a relationship with
your consumers. In Nigeria, or across the continent where we
distribute books, the readers read your book and immediately
are there right in your face, telling you about it. If they don't get
their books delivered [on time], they are talking to you; you
can build a community around the company. The challenges
also come with the reward.

**Joel Cabrita:** It sounds like such a dense compacted world in which boundaries between publisher, printer, distributor, reader, and reviewer are all collapsed. There are so many points I'd like to pick up on but I'm just going to ask one final question and then throw it open to the students. In a talk you gave in 2018, you used the term 'colonial linguistic capture'. Could you speak more specifically to the issue of language? As far as I'm aware, Cassava Republic publishes largely or solely in English. Of course, as you know this is a long-standing debate among African publishers and writers about publishing in English versus publishing in indigenous African languages. We've already had a conversation with Ellah Wakatama in this forum, and her reply was that obviously English is an African language. Could you speak to us about how you approach this question?

**Bibi Bakare-Yusuf:** You know, it's a bit like when [Chinua] Achebe says, 'I am going to do wonders with the English language'[1]. Ellah is in that tradition of [seeing] English as an African language. I'm totally on the opposite end of that. English is a European language – it is not African. Africans use English precisely because of the colonial encounter and English is a reminder of the violence of the encounter and of the fact that we have – whether we like it or not – been subjugated. We inflect it with our traditions, and we may do all kinds of amazingness and wonders with the English language, but ultimately what we are doing is helping to enrich the English language to the impoverishment of our own languages.

At Cassava Republic, I'm acutely aware that we publish in

---

[1] 'Let no one be fooled by the fact that we may write in English, for we intend to do unheard of things with it' – Chinua Achebe.

English precisely because of colonial capture. What is colonial capture? Colonization is not just physical colonization based on commerce and economy. It is also cultural colonization. The greatest violence of that encounter is the linguistic one. And it's [paradoxically] the linguistic violence that has enabled all of us today to talk across our differences. On one level, it is great that we can converse [in English] as we may come from different linguistic backgrounds, different ethnic groups. But English is still a colonizing language, and we cannot escape that. By bringing Yoruba or isiZulu into English, all I'm doing is making English richer, helping the [English] language become more supple and survive. I am ensuring its longevity. [Yet] what am I doing with Yoruba? What am I doing with isiZulu? What am I doing with Swahili? Am I bringing all the knowledge, all the dynamism of English back into those languages? We're not. Today many languages are dying out in Nigeria precisely because of colonial capture.

I recommend all of you to read Mukoma wa Ngũgĩ's book, *The Rise of the African Novel*, where he talks about the English metaphysical empire. We don't think about writing in African languages because we think it's a done deal that English is 'it'. But I don't think [the dominance of English is] a fait accompli. I think it's something that we have to keep wrestling with. We have to not take it for granted. And this is why I would never think that English is an African language. To accept this is to forget the violence and the continued violence of Englishness. The day I will accept that English is an African language will be my final acceptance of our complete colonization and the impossibility of complete decolonization.

**Joel Cabrita:** It's fascinating to see your two positions at opposite ends of the spectrum.

**Bibi Bakare-Yusuf:** It is the Achebe and the Ngũgĩ [wa Thiong'o] position. Ellah occupies the Achebe position and I occupy the Ngũgĩ position. Unfortunately for both of us, we're working through the body of the fathers. You could even characterize it in terms of Martin Luther King versus Malcolm X in America. I probably occupy the Malcolm X end of the spectrum, not really Martin Luther King.

**Anita Too:** Thank you, this is so engaging. I could listen to you speaking for hours and hours. One of the questions we've been grappling with in this class is what exactly is African literature? There's a burden for a lot of African writers whereby [they are expected to] be illustrative, to show the white world what 'Africa' is. So writers are relegated to tour guides, showing readers that Africans don't do this, Africans do this. I'm curious when you're looking at texts, what do you as a publishing house use to determine how you class something as African?

**Bibi Bakare-Yusuf:** Even though most of the books that we have published are by writers from continental Africa, our mission as a publishing house is a broader notion of Africa, whether on the continent or within the diaspora. And I think you've captured the very thing that I'm against – which is the burden for African writers or Black writers to make themselves legible to another society or another culture. I'm not interested in publishing books that are trying to explain who we are to somebody else. I'm interested in texts that first and foremost try to show us to ourselves, anew. I'm interested in texts that bring the mundane aspects of who we are into focus and make them grander for us to see and to marvel at. And the text doesn't have to be set on the continent. It could be set anywhere. It could be about any subject. I'm not interested in any restrictions as to how you write. What I'm interested in is how are you handling your craft? What are you doing that allows us to look at ourselves as human beings, what new insights are you creating? Are your stories going to shed light for people in 300 years' time about what is happening today?

Books are like food, and the things that we eat can either nourish or poison us. What we have as Black people has been a situation where we have been used to looking out of the window. Yet, if you think about a child growing up, that child also needs to look at itself in the mirror. European children grew up looking in the mirror all the time. There's a certain narcissism about how Europeans are groomed. It breeds a certain conquering spirit as well. On the other hand, Black people have been groomed to look out of the window, all the time. We're constantly looking out of the window and trying to project what we see outside back onto ourselves. What we need is both. We need to be able to look at ourselves in the mirror and return love to ourselves and marvel at our own beauty. But we also need to look out of the window to see the world of others so we can have empathy. These two things make us human, fully rounded people. So, I'm interested in literature that is internal, but is also an invitation to see the world and to be in conversation with each other. Thank you, Anita, for that wonderful question.

**Brittany Linus:** It's very interesting when you talk about looking out of a window and into a mirror. W.E.B. Du Bois coins this as double consciousness. As Black Americans, we look at ourselves as Black people but also as Americans. And these two identities are constantly in a battle with each other, because as a Black American, America doesn't like you. But you are a Black person, and you want to love yourself. But you also have to remember that the world does not love you back. I am Black, but I'm also American and I have to be conscious of the ways in which I present myself. For example, I'm a Black woman. If I'm passionate about something, [America] will see me as a Black woman who is angry and violent.

**Bibi Bakare-Yusuf:** When I was in boarding school in England, people would ask me questions like, 'Do you guys live in trees in Nigeria?' And the thing that I had going for me as a Black person in England was this: I know you. I know you as a white English person. I know you and I know me. So, I'm already at an advantage. You will never be able to know me, you'll only ever be able to know yourself. I'm always going to have a leg up over you. This double consciousness is an enabling power that we can use for our own purpose. Because I'm conscious of it, I have a double perspective. I can see you coming before you can see yourself coming because I'm working dialectically.

**Katlo Gasewagae:** I agree with you that one cannot build a civilization on a diet of John Grisham, and self-help books like *Rich Dad, Poor Dad*. Can you talk more about the idea of building a civilization, and how that has informed your decision to start a publishing company? As a publisher, do you feel responsible for the task of world making for Africans by Africans and if so, why?

Also, even though there are myriad of stories out there in the ether, the stories that get rewarded by institutions like book prizes seem to be the ones that feed into stereotypes about Africa – the poverty of the continent, needing a white saviour and so on. What is your opinion on institutions like book prizes? Do they have a responsibility to be more intentional about the works they reward?

**Bibi Bakare-Yusuf:** Wonderful, smart question, thank you. I think you've answered your own question. We only ascribe value to what the Booker Prize tells us, or what the Pen/ Hemingway Award tells us. We cannot expect those people to change because their prizes were never designed with us in mind. As Black people, we've been forcing our way into those spaces. Sometimes you need to take your chair to the table and sit at the table and have your dinner. At other times, you've got to make up your own table. What I'm trying to do is to make our own table so that we can say to ourselves that the table we've set up is enough. The same values that we ascribe to publishing with Random House we should eventually ascribe to publishing with Cassava Republic.

When I set up Cassava Republic, I wanted to control the means of production. I'm just as solipsistic as those white publishing companies are. I want power, just like them. I understand the importance of power and what power does in our lives, and the ways in which we need to wrestle with power especially as women, and especially as Black people. We need to do our own stuff, and to be the people who own the means of production, who own educational capital, financial capital, cultural capital, social capital. All these things put together become symbolic capital. The power of whiteness and the power of the awarding bodies is [that] they have symbolic legitimacy. We don't have the symbolic legitimacy yet. We have to start building those bases, and that starts in education. We also need economic power. We talk about Black Lives Matter. Black lives will continue to not matter in the eyes of whiteness and ourselves because we don't have the economic base, especially on the continent. We need all these different types of capital so that we can truly make decisions about who gets awards, who contributes to civilization or not.

And when I think about civilization, I think about the artefacts that we will leave behind us, our habits of being, our ways of doing things, the food and drink we consume, the stories, the language, and the metaphors we use. These are all part of the things that form civilization. And I want to contribute to that. In 500 years' time when we want to talk about how people think about love, let's pick up one of our books. So let's proliferate stories by Africans, by Black people. Let's saturate the world's archives with books written and produced by Black people. At the moment, the written archives of Black people are very thin relative to our size and our time on this planet. I want us to have literary texts in saturated quantities, to match our population size relative to the world's population. And by Black people I mean whether we are in or from Alabama or Angola, in Congo or Cuba, I want us to have more of those multiple stories.

**Joel Cabrita:** Is it worth thinking about the continued strength of historically white institutions, both in publishing and in scholarship about publishing? What do you think about, for example, the fact these conversations are being hosted by a university in the Global North?

**Bibi Bakare-Yusuf:** This speaks to precisely my point above –

as long as economic power resides in whiteness, what you're saying will continue to be the case. Black people's encounter with other Black people will be mediated by whiteness. And for me that's not an interesting conversation. What we need is a broader conversation around structure, around institutions, as opposed to individual power dynamics – which of course are part of the building blocks of structures and institutions. How do we dismantle the structures that continue to make that possible? That's what I'm interested in, in the same way that I'm interested in how we build structures for Black people. The conversation we need to be having is about the structure of power, especially within a university setting. How many Black people are employed within academia? How many Black people do PhDs and stay in academia? Those are more interesting and urgent conversations than focusing on a single white person's ownership and access to power and resources.

**Joel Cabrita:** You mention what you call the Euro-American publishing industrial complex – that is to say, the strength of the publishing industry in Western Europe and North America. Can you tell us more about your decision to go into the heart of it now that you've opened up an office of Cassava Republic in London? I saw you mentioning that you would also like to do that in the USA. How do you see the future of Cassava outside of the African continent?

**Bibi Bakare-Yusuf:** We made a decision to go back to England and set up an office there because, whether we like it or not, London, New York, Paris – these are still the centres of empire. I always remind people that we're not in a post-colonial moment. We're in a new colonial moment. We're going back to the heart of Empire, to have a conversation with Empire. Why should it be that the Empire is always coming to Africa to set up office? Let's go and set up office there and see what we can get from there. That's reason number one [for having an office there].

Reason number two, it's precisely because of the colonial project that so many Africans are conversing with each other through these nodes of power, through these colonial centres. We all meet in London; we all meet in New York. We're not meeting in Kinshasa, we're not meeting in Johannesburg, we're not meeting in Lagos. There's nothing we can do about it, for now. For me to speak to and engage with my African-American sisters, my Jamaican sisters, London is a lot more accessible than just simply being based in Abuja. So, it's pragmatic.

The aim is also to inject a certain fever into the British publishing landscape, to say [to them] that these periodic feel-good things that you do – you publish one or two Black people every year and you clap for yourself – are not enough. We want to be able to create a home for Black people. The fact of the matter is that most Black people don't necessarily want to publish with Cassava Republic or rather we are not always their first choice. That is the reality of being a conquered people and I am aware of this, and I don't delude myself otherwise. There are Black people who don't want to publish with us because they think, 'I don't want to be in a ghetto'. But they forget that you're already in the ghetto of and within whiteness if you go with Penguin Random House or such. But there are a few who actively want to be published by us and choose us as their first choice. Either way, I embrace our nervous condition as a people!

**Katlo Gasewagae:** I'm intrigued by how you talk about capital and power, and the need to have it in certain hands. The idea that Africans need power, and they need capital in order to be able to negotiate at the global level. I agree with you. But at the same time, you can't use the very same tools that are used to oppress you to get out of oppression. I wonder what your thoughts are about that.

**Bibi Bakare-Yusuf:** It's a question that I wrestle with a lot. I'm anti-capitalist. Let's not confuse thinking about capital with capitalism, because I think you can command capital without it being within the unequal, unjust capitalist framework. So, my demand for power doesn't necessarily have to go along the same journey as the existing structure. For example, as a publisher my philosophy is that within the company the payment structure between the person who's earning the most, and the person who's earning the lowest, the distance must not be so huge. As Black people, as Africans, we must take economic power seriously. We must think about how we fashion equity, wealth that's inclusive and that allows us to carry most of our people with us. Anything else, an amassing of excess wealth, is theft. Ultimately, it robs the majority.

**Brittany Linus:** When you were talking about African or Black writers who don't want to publish with an African publishing company, it brought me back to that detached art debate that Langston Hughes often commented on. You can only write based upon your own experience and you can only write therefore based upon your own Black experience. With regard to this capitalist question, can you redeem those tools of oppression and turn them into something else?

**Bibi Bakare-Yusuf:** No. They are tools of oppression, that's what they're there for. This goes back to what I said at the beginning about language, and about whether English can be an African language. It's a European language, let's keep it at that. And the tools of oppression – they are instruments of oppression. I can use this hand to soothe, and I can use it to punch. But why should we recoup tools of oppression? Why not create new tools for what we need? That's for me a much more interesting undertaking, because to redeem the tools of oppression for liberty is going to take work. So why not just start the work of fashioning a new tool altogether? It is laziness, on our part, that we want to continue to use the tools of oppression that have not served us. Also, when you continue to use the tool of oppression, there will be a kind of return of the repressed, it will come back to haunt us in new and unpredictable ways. You might as well start something afresh. That's what I tried to do with starting Cassava Republic. We could have looked for a Western company and said to them, 'Come to Africa, come set up here'. And to what purpose? They will only bring their baggage and all their systems with them. So, let's fashion a new one. Let's make all the mistakes – and believe me, I'm very concerned about all those we have made. I've made lots of huge, costly mistakes, and I will continue to make them. You make mistakes when you're building institutions. The difference is that for Black people, especially for Black women, we're not allowed to make mistakes because we're having to fashion institutions in full gaze of others who had a head start of 500 or 700 years to do that fashioning themselves and make mistakes along the way. That's the problem and then we end up self-sabotaging, attacking ourselves for getting things wrong. People don't allow us to grow, to make mistakes, to take baby steps. That's what we need. I talk a lot about the importance of critical tenderness. We need to be gentle on ourselves, we need not be so harsh on ourselves.

**About Bibi Bakare-Yusuf:** Bibi is the publishing director of Cassava Republic Press – a publishing company she co-founded in 2006, in Abuja, Nigeria. In 2014 she created Ankara Books, an associated imprint that focused on modern African romance novels. Bibi is also an independent scholar. She was elected an honorary fellow of the Royal Society of Literature in 2019 and she has also been a Yale World Fellow, a Desmond Tutu Fellow, and a Frankfurt Book Fair Fellow.

*'This is something that I've dreamt
of for a very long time – where we, as an
African continent, start to speak to each other
across language barriers.'*

## IN CONVERSATION WITH:
## ZUKISWA WANNER

3 March 2021

**Joel Cabrita:** Let's begin with your biography. Tell us about yourself and tell us what led you to writing and into literature.

**Zukiswa Wanner:** I studied journalism in Hawaii and after that I went to work in the UK. I stayed there for a bit and then my dad died. Just as a bit of background for you, my dad is South African. My mom is Zimbabwean, and I was born in Zambia. And now I stay in Kenya sometimes. But yeah, my dad died and I took leave and went to South Africa for the funeral, and then I returned to the UK. Two days after returning, I went to Flight Centre, bought my ticket back to South Africa, and I told my boss that I was leaving.

He said 'What?' and I replied 'I'm leaving. I'm going back to South Africa on Friday.' (It was a Wednesday.) He then said, 'Well, you know you have to work a month's notice.' And I said 'Well, how about you notice that I'm not here for the next month?' So, I left and went to South Africa. Everything was so vibrant back then in 2003. There was an air of hope, and that we could do anything and be anything. Then I started looking for a job and I couldn't find one. One day I was volunteering at a community-based organization which worked with HIV/ AIDS orphans. We were trying to get them birth certificates and get them into schools, that sort of thing. It was then I met the late great photographer, Alf Kumalo. As usual, he had his Nikon camera around his neck. Seeing him I thought, maybe I need to pad up my CV with photography so that I can get a job. So I asked him. Imagine my pleasant surprise when he told me he had set up a photographic school and museum in Diepkloof and was looking for students? So I immediately arranged to visit the next day and he agreed.

I don't know what made me take my journalism portfolio with me, but when I got there, the school was working with some Italian arts organization and its coordinator who was also there went through my portfolio and he said, 'Listen, I know you came here looking for classes but we really need a PR person. Can you do it?' I said 'Yeah, sure.' Unfortunately, not a lot of people used to come to this museum although I used to get paid every month regardless. But one of the people who came through was the late Lewis Nkosi, who wrote *Mating Birds*. He was also a literary critic of sorts. We started chatting and he gave me his email address. I asked him if he could possibly look at some of my writing. He was indulgent enough to agree and so I sent him some stuff and he started reading it, and he said, 'You know, you should write fiction.' I said, 'I'm too much of a realist to write fiction.' And he said, 'That's the greatest bullshit I ever heard.' I ignored him. Then a few months later he was down in Joburg, and I bumped into him at Joburg Arts Gallery. He introduced me to somebody there, saying, 'This is one of the greatest young writers we have in the country today.' This guy gave me his card and told me to send him my stuff. I did.

He emailed me after a few days and he said to me, 'You really should consider writing fiction.' This guy is an essayist, so I don't know if that meant my creative nonfiction wasn't that great [laughs]. Anyway, I took that as a challenge and over the course of two to three weeks I wrote the first draft of *The Madams*. I didn't have my own computer, so I was writing it at work because it was so boring there that there was little for me to do. After I'd finished it, I didn't think it was anything. I sent it to this old man, the late Basil 'Doc' Bikitsha who was a friend of mine, a retired journalist, and he read it. He called me and said, 'Baby! Baby! This is some gooood shit!' And I said, 'Okaay.' Then he said, 'I'm sending my driver with some notes, things that I think you need to change. Read those notes, make the changes, and send it to these five publishers.' So that's essentially what I did. I looked at what he said, I took notes, and I did the editorial changes, sent it to five publishers and three of them accepted it. So you can say in this way that my literary life was rather charmed. And then I selected the one who I thought was for me. And that's the backstory.

**Joel Cabrita:** On the topic of *The Madams*, we read and discussed it in class. One of the things that came up was this issue of the label 'chick lit', because that's often attached to you and your work. We were thinking about the complexities of that label. How do you feel about it? Is it something you embrace? Is it a label that you think should be consigned to the dustbin of history?

**Zukiswa Wanner:** I actually think it's a rubbish label to be honest. The biggest book buyers are women, you know. But also, chick lit as opposed to what? Penis lit? Dick lit? What's the parallel to chick lit, you know? The other thing is I think it's a way of ghettoizing stuff. But getting that particular label has always challenged me to do other things with my work. After I wrote *The Madams*, I wanted to do a reply from a male perspective and so I wrote *Men of the South* and then nobody ever called it dick lit. I was so sad.

**Joel Cabrita:** Yeah, so clearly there's some kind of double standard at play whereby women's writing is put into its own category and those exclusive labels don't operate for men's work.

**Zukiswa Wanner:** Well, not just women's writing. It's women's writing when women are writing about women, because nobody said that when I was writing about these three male protagonists in *Men of the South*.

**Joel Cabrita:** Also on the topic of *The Madams*, let's talk about language. One of the topics that has come up with a lot of the guests that we've had over the past weeks has been the issue of language and what languages writers choose to use for their work. Obviously, all of your work to my knowledge is written in English. Talk to us about that. We'd love to know where you position yourself in this debate about African languages versus English or French or colonial languages more broadly.

**Zukiswa Wanner:** I see English, Portuguese, and French as African languages. Everyone here in this [Zoom] room is from a different country. Yet we all can understand each other because we're speaking English. In fact, you probably wouldn't have even invited me to this class if I had written a book in isiXhosa, which is my dad's language, or Shona, which is my mom's language because the only people who would have been able to access it are people who speak that language. That said, I am generally the type of person who believes that an artist should create in whatever colours they want to create in, so if somebody is more comfortable with writing in Dholuo for instance or in Nyanja or in Bemba or in Yoruba, they should go ahead. But there is also the other work that needs to be done. For instance, when I published the children's books. This was an anthology called *Story, Story! Story, Come!* It has a Xhosa translation because it was very important to me that not just children who speak English have access to it because I think they are really good stories. I also did a Shona translation (I did that translation myself, so I have written in another language). I've also published a TshiVenda translation and a Kiswahili translation, but that's not yet out. I think my duty as a publisher would then be to say that because I love something so much, I want it to be accessible in other languages. But my duty as a writer is different. When I'm a writer, I'm an artist, and as an artist I should be able to write in whatever language I'm comfortable in, but in a language that I feel that can reach as many people as possible. As my literary mother Ama Ata Aidoo liked saying, 'I don't understand the argument about writing in English for Africans because our ancestors were killed for that language.'

Of course, you will have noticed when you were reading *The Madams* that I did put certain very South African, very African, phrases in the text, as I do with all my texts. This is something that Shimmer Chinodya likes saying and I like playing with this and quoting it a lot: 'It's called colonizing the colonial language'. Doing with it what you will. I enjoy doing that. And so sometimes I think it's a nod nod wink wink to people from the Global South because there are certain things that I know only they would understand. For instance, in a lot of African languages you don't walk a lot, you walk and walk and walk and walk and walk. You also hear the smell, you know. There are these little things that I always feel when I'm reading a book. It's like 'Aaaah, you're talking to *me*!'

**Joel Cabrita:** I notice how you differentiate between your roles as an artist and as a publisher and see the responsibilities of each as different. You wear so many different hats: you're not only a writer but you're also a publisher, you're also a literary judge, you're also the founder of an online literary festival. So, we'd like to hear more about those other roles that you occupy alongside writing. Let's begin by talking about your publishing company, Paivapo, which you founded in 2018.

**Zukiswa Wanner:**  Yes, December 2018 was when our first book came out. Because I'd been working with publishers and a lot of my stuff was published by South African publishers, I found there were certain things that I thought were missing from the South African scene. Things I thought I could bridge the gap with. For instance, my South African publisher was very excited to take my book to London or the Frankfurt Book Fair. They would send me an excited email when somebody from Germany, France or the UK or the US was talking about the fact that they'd read my work and they were wondering if they could publish it. But the publisher didn't show as much of a keen interest when somebody from Nigeria or from Ghana or from Malawi said the same thing.

Yet these were the people that I was talking to. I had deliberately gone to these countries as far back as 2008, making deliberate trips to other African countries and I would take my books with me. I'd maybe know one person and I'd be like, 'How can we have a reading?' type of thing. People were very receptive to that because they were like, 'Oh wow, this is our story.' Some of them had last read a book in high school, when they had read *Things Fall Apart*.

Then my friend from Gambia who was then also staying in Nairobi, Maimouna Jallow-Vulart, got in touch with me to ask me to publish this children's anthology because she knew I had just set up a publishing company. I was ambivalent about it. But I am indulgent with my friends so I asked her to send it and told her if I liked it, we would make a plan. She sent it. I liked it. I liked it so much that I wrote a bonus story for the anthology. And she had managed to secure funding for it so she gave me the East and Southern African publishing rights and Lola Shoneyin's Ouida Books the West African publishing rights. That's how I published my first book. I didn't think that I'd ever publish a children's book when I started, but there, you know, life happens. So I did the children's book and then the second book came to me by accident, actually. I had run out of books to read. And I had Mukoma wa Ngugi's *Mrs Shaw*. Mukoma is a friend of mine, so of course I had bought the book. But it wasn't an inspiring title – Mrs Shaw – and I hadn't yet read it. So now I was like, 'Ah! Now I have nothing to read. Let me just read this *Mrs Shaw* book that's there.' And I read it. And when I read, I thought, 'Oh my! This as far as I'm concerned is the best book that Mukoma has written.' I wanted to invite him for my Artistic Encounters series.[1] He was published by Ohio University Press but when I asked them for copies, they told me that they didn't have any. And then I said to them, 'Okay, can I buy the rights for Africa?' And they said to me, 'Yeah sure, you can buy the rights.' I bought the Africa rights from them and of course I had to do some edits as well in it because… I don't know man, Americans just tend to spell tyre for cars as t-i-r-e instead of t-y-r-e so things like that had to be changed. And then I wanted to play with other things like reformatting the emails in the book to fit in with the timeframe they should have been written. So perhaps a mailcity or hotmail email address as opposed to the more recent Google.

When we finished that, I got a whole new cover and then I told Mukoma that we needed a change of title. It couldn't be *Mrs Shaw* as I couldn't sell *Mrs Shaw* to this continent. More so given how long it had taken me to read the book because of the title despite being Mukoma's friend. So Mukoma and I started playing around with ideas. One day when I was in the swimming pool, I came up with this title. And I talked to Mukoma, and said, *'How about We the Scarred?'* Because the story has a character who leaves his own country, a fictional African country. He's escaping because he was fighting for democracy under a dictatorship and before he left, he had been arrested and beaten. So now he goes to the US and every now and again he has these nightmares, and he scratches himself and he's got these scars. But the people that he left behind are also scarred. So there are these scars, these conflicts about who is more injured, who deserves a place at the table and is truth

---

[1]   Artistic Encounters, founded by Wanner, brings together the work of two different artists in the same space, at the same time.

more important than reconciliation. After I read it, I thought that this could be anywhere-ville in the Global South. It could be Brazil, it could be South Africa, it could be Nigeria, it could be Congo. Anywhere, it could be anywhere, like the Philippines. So that's what I did with that. It came out last year and of course Mukoma and I had planned on a wonderful launch idea where he was going to do a launch in Joburg and then we'd meet in Kigali. Then we'd do a road trip where we'd read both our works: Kigali, Kampala, Eldoret, Kisumu, Nakuru and then end up with Nairobi. But yeah, Lord, Covid happened.

**Joel Cabrita:** Covid happened.

**Zukiswa Wanner:** This year I have two projects coming up. One is a book by Nokuthula Msimang which is a reimagining of Nandi, the mother of Shaka (*Daughters of Nandi* has been out since December 2021 and has been well received across the continent). The other one is something that I'm equally excited about. I got the rights to translate and publish Yara Monteiro's novel. She is an Angolan writer. This is something that I've dreamed of for a very long time – where we as an African continent start to speak to each other across language barriers (this was published in 2021 as *Loose Ties* and has been equally well received. Yara has been invited to a few literary festivals on the continent in English-speaking Africa because of it). And of course, I'm very excited that *The Madams* is also being translated by a Mozambican and Angolan publisher into Portuguese. So there's that.

**Olayinka Adekola:** My question goes back to how you said that you colonized the colonizer as well as the colonizing language.

We've been talking about African-American Vernacular English in class and I certainly feel that it has become an African language. Do you feel that colonizing the colonizer's language only has an impact on the African language, or also on the English language? Do you think it enriches the English language or do you think it helps to make a way for African-speaking people to navigate the English language? What do you view as the impact of that process?

**Zukiswa Wanner:** Thanks for that question, Ola. I actually think it enriches the English language because I think there are many Englishes. I think there is an English that is spoken in Malaysia and that people in Singapore also speak and understand. One of my favourite books is Eghosa Imasuen's *Fine Boy*. He writes it entirely in Nigerian Pidgin and I think Pidgin is a language on its own because it is the one language spoken by everyone in Nigeria. People speak Yoruba, people speak Igbo, people speak Hausa, but Pidgin is the one language that unites everybody, you know? If you are not so familiar with Nigeria and just coming into the country, you'll be like, 'What did you just say?' But Nigerians will understand. And people in the region will understand. And of course, I think quite a lot of Africans now understand it because, hey, we are all watching Nollywood [laughs].

**Michelle Julia Ng:** How else has Covid affected the way that you've gone about your work, both as a writer and also as a publisher? Where do you see this going forward?

**Zukiswa Wanner:** Well, the road trip. That was obviously disappointing not to do. But a few days after Kenya went into lockdown on 17 March 2020, we actually started a new literary platform, a literary festival called Afrolit Sans Frontières. And to me it was very exciting, curating this new platform and getting all these writers together. The very first Afrolit Sans Frontières theme was sex. You always have these ignorant statements from people who don't read enough, they will say stuff like, 'Oh, you know, uh, African writers don't write about sex, African writers don't write about humour.' So I wanted to use that space to show people that yes, contemporary African writers are writing about all sorts of things. They are writing science fiction, writing crime fiction, they're writing humour and so forth. And, I think we did that. We did five seasons. The last season was just focused on African languages. And I think it was successful. It managed to make the point. Importantly, we managed to speak across languages again, across borders, because we did the festival in English, French and Portuguese. So we got our siblings from Francophone Africa and from Lusophone Africa to be part of that festival. And we respected them enough not to expect them to translate for us. So we kind of got the gist of what people were saying. Also, I would not have met Yara, who I am now publishing in English translating from Portuguese, if it wasn't because we'd had a lockdown and she became part of Afrolit Sans Frontières through another friend of mine Kalaf Epalanga. And Ondjaki told me about her, to invite her, so that is how I got to know her and then became curious about her work. So I think there were opportunities that Covid brought.

**Joel Cabrita:** How did you choose the name Afrolit Sans Frontières? Because I think of Medecins Sans Frontières…

**Zukiswa Wanner:** That's it. That is actually what I was thinking about. Abubakar Ibrahim and I had a conversation about it on a Friday, early Friday morning, maybe at 2 a.m. He said it's a great idea. And when I woke up the next morning, I started sending messages to everybody. I'm like, 'Who wants to be part of this? Let's have a festival starting on Monday.' It was all very sudden. The first fifteen people [I asked] said yes. I was like, yes! So on Friday, I'd already hit my line-up. Then on Saturday, I thought, 'Oh, flip, what am I going to call this?' I thought, 'Well, African literature without borders. So, Afrolit Sans Frontières.'

**Barry Migott:** You talk of this cross-pollination of ideas across the continent and as a publisher, you're engaging with writers across the continent. One of our prior guests, Bibi Bakare-Yusuf, is a publisher partly based in London. When we asked her about her choice of locating her company abroad, she talked about it being easier for African writers to converge in London compared to converging in an African country. So what influenced your decision to base your publishing house on the continent?

**Zukiswa Wanner:** I have to disagree with Bibi on that one, unless you're looking at African writers in the diaspora. Certainly a festival like Ake, which is one of the biggest festivals that everybody wants to attend, in Lagos, Nigeria, brings together many amazing people from all over the world. In fact, last year the festival was online and names like Tayari Jones, Mukoma wa Ngũgĩ, Mona Eltahawy, Maaza Mengiste, were all there... everyone you could think of! So I'm not entirely sure about [what Bibi says]. But it also depends on who she, as a publisher, is trying to market to. I have made a very deliberate choice as a publisher to speak to the continent. I know that Ake festival exists. I know there is the amazing Hargeysa festival in Somaliland, The Gaborone festival is brilliant, in DR Congo there's Fête du livre. Ghana also has the Paa Gya festival. So there is a lot of stuff happening on the continent. Maybe because Bibi doesn't stay on the continent all the time, she might sometimes miss things. But I stay here. And I try to visit at least one other African country that I haven't been to every year. In each country, I always see that there is a vibrant literary community. In certain places it's smaller than in others. One of the most exciting literary magazines coming out of this continent is *Doek*, from Namibia (they now have a Doek Literary Festival which is absolutely stunning). Now, Namibia has like five people, five [laughs]! One of my friends says – obviously it would be a Nigerian friend – that Namibia and Botswana don't need presidents, they need mayors, you know, because their populations are so small. So there are a lot of exciting things happening.

**Katlo Gasewagae:** I'm glad that we've moved to talking about festivals because I think that Afrolit Sans Frontières is such a fitting attempt to answer our earlier discussion on the question of access, especially during Covid. The festival is online and it's free so you don't have to pay in order to jump in and take part. I would like to ask, though, who is your viewership for the festival? And are you reaching the kind of audience that you would like to reach? As you mentioned, you want to speak to the continent and you want African people in Africa to understand the vibrant literary culture that already exists on the continent. This is a question that can be extrapolated even to publishing houses and the books that are published all across

Africa. Do you see these books reaching the people who need them, or is it the stereotypical case with capitalism, that it's usually people who don't have to negotiate access who tend to get access to them?

**Zukiswa Wanner:** With Afrolit Sans Frontières, it was the privileged who have data, who have that access. But part of the reason I made sure that we have an archive of the festival on YouTube is because I hope, at a later date, for it to become a resource for schools, for universities, where people will have access to it. So you don't need to have [personal] data, but if you're in university like Makerere [in Uganda] or University of Botswana, you can get into a space where your teacher can be able to put it online, and then you're able to see it. With regard to books that I publish, one of the things that I am very deliberately working on with a lot of my friends, including the Gaborone Book Festival, for instance, is this (holds up *Story, Story! Story, Come!*) in the English version. They are distributing it to schools in the far-flung areas in Botswana. We are also in conversation with them about having a Setswana translation so that children in Botswana can get it in their language. It's part of the reason why I started with the translation process. The second thing is I'm working with a Zimbabwean guy in Australia who is an engineer. He loves books and he started setting up libraries in rural Zimbabwe. His NGO buys books in Shona, and then I find some funding from whatever places that I can. We'll get artists to do audio recordings of the stories and then these stories can reach into these rural, rural, rural places that have never had a library. So there's an audio version of the story. They'll supply a computer, and make sure they employ a librarian from the village so that she has an income and she'll help the slower kids listen to the story with headphones so they can follow it. This is a way of helping literacy as well, because you can't talk about literature without talking about literacy. It's not divorced. I've been talking to Open Society in Southern Africa hoping that within the next year we can at least have a few pilot programmes. Again, Covid stopped us from doing this, but I would like to see whether I can push it in different spaces across the continent.

**Chepchirchir Tirop:** I'm so amazed by all these ideas that are coming up, especially the translation. I've been trying to read a book from every African country and I was stuck with Central African Republic because I could not find a single Anglophone translation of any book. In connection to that, I noticed when you were speaking about the different African languages that you did not mention Arabic. How do you think about North Africa as part of the African landscape?

**Zukiswa Wanner:** I do certainly think that Arabic and North Africa are part of the African continent, but the truth of the matter is Arabic is more widely translated than even English on this continent. There are so many resources that the Middle East has put in translating Arabic. So I don't think they really need my help, I need their help.

**Chepchirchir Tirop:** I hear that 100 per cent. Also, how do you see the relationship between the literary landscape and higher educational institutions? I was just reading an article recently about how syllabi in different universities, both on the continent and abroad, perpetuate a very specific idea of what African literature is and what it should do. So I was wondering how we think about that relationship and maybe also your role as a publisher and as a writer?

**Zukiswa Wanner:** I think some universities are better than others. Part of the problem is that a lot of lecturers are underpaid. We are a continent that pays MPs more than we pay academics. So academics will be using the same syllabus from twenty years ago. They don't need to put any effort into it, because nobody is paying them enough. Nobody really cares about how well they do their thing. There's a need for writers and academics to talk to each other. That has been happening quite a bit lately. I've seen it. That's also part of the reason that I was chatting to Joel earlier and asking her whether we would have a recording of these sessions available for free so that African academics can have access to them. This is something really, really, really close to my heart. I refuse to do any events with Columbia University because they say people would need to pay to access the platform. They could be available for them online, but they would need to pay afterwards. And I'm like, 'Come on, man! You've got one of the biggest endowments [in the US], you can afford to give these things for free, but you don't want to.' So I say to them, 'No, I'm not doing the event.' And I refused it. We have to be very deliberate as the literati. [Somali novelist] Nuruddin Farah is doing something very exciting. He is actually archiving and interviewing his writer friends from his own generation and making those conversations available. I think that's exciting. We have to be very deliberate about it because I don't want in thirty years' time, for somebody who is an African scholar to have to pay a university in the US for information about my work. It's rubbish.

**Joel Cabrita:** Thank you so much, very powerful. We had Ellah Wakatama speak to us and she said something that I think is comparable to what you're saying, which is as students, if you're confronted with syllabi on courses, that for example, don't feature the work of any Black or African scholars, or just lots of white men, then speak up. You can use your voice to say that this is unacceptable. So it's similar to what you were saying about refusing speaking engagements with certain institutions which don't have an open access platform. It's an inspiring message about an individual's capacity to change things. We're out of time, so Zukiswa, is there anything that you would like to talk about that we haven't addressed here?

**Zukiswa Wanner:** Um, I just wanted to let you know that my t-shirt says, 'Fuck Google, ask me.' And sometimes it's much better to ask the people on the ground than to make assumptions from 'experts' who are not immersed in the issues.

**Katlo Gasewagae:** Thank you for that. I love it even more now.

**About Zukiswa Wanner:** Zukiswa is the author of four novels, three children's books and two works of nonfiction. Zukiswa is the founder and curator of Artistic Encounters, Afrolit Sans Frontières and Virtually Yours and one third of Writer's Inc. Zukiswa is also a co-founder of independent publishing house, Paivapo. In 2015, Zukiswa won the K Sello Duiker Memorial Literary Award for her book *London Cape Town Joburg* (2014).

*'I want to hold onto the utopian possibility that social media allows us to right the wrongs of history by putting Africa at the centre.'*

# IN CONVERSATION WITH: AINEHI EDORO

10 March 2021

**Joel Cabrita:** So – just to begin with a biographical question – tell us about where your passion for African literature came from and the early influences that shaped you.

**Ainehi Edoro:** Nice to meet everybody. I appreciate you all having me here to talk about my work. At a very young age, I realized that African literature was something special. It wasn't just something that I studied in school. So I wanted to pursue a career in it, either as a fiction writer or by being involved in literature in some other way. In college, I realized that there is something called a 'scholar'. Scholars don't write novels, but they say smart things about novels that other people have written. That just felt way more fun. It's like you play around in the archive and you read whatever you want and then you say things. I decided to pursue a career in literary academia. But I also realized that although it was wonderful, I still wanted something different. That's how *Brittle Paper* came about.

**Joel Cabrita:** Tell us about the name. How did you come upon *Brittle Paper*? Why did you choose to call your platform that?

**Ainehi Edoro:** It is 2009: the height of the blogging universe. Blogging allowed people to create an audience around ranting about personal things. There was something about this aspect of digital culture that attracted me: the way in which it could fragment life into little things in interesting ways. That has stayed with me in my study of digital culture — this obsession with small things that can collectively accumulate to very meaningful and impactful things. There was also something about the fragility that came with that and the fact that suddenly fragility isn't something bad. It's okay if I write something, somebody sees it in a minute, it disappears and nobody sees it again. There's nothing inherently bad about that. This is not the classic literary world where there is an obsession with longevity. We obsess over classics because they've been around for 200 years. Social media and web culture are different; it is the opposite. Somehow, digital culture can create meaning and value and form out of things that are tiny and appear for a flicker of the moment and disappear. I loved that. The idea of brittleness, of fragility, of ephemerality as being the ground for meaning and form was one of the initial ways in which I was trying to conceptualize what this project was going to be. That's where the name *Brittle Paper* comes from.

**Joel Cabrita:** When you mentioned fragmentation, I not only thought about ephemerality, but also more recent critiques about social media. These critiques have addressed the older tech-utopianism: the notion that social media would unite us, forming new global solidarities and really capacious collective identities. But somehow the opposite seems to have happened: social media instead seems to fragment people into small interest groups, gathered in our little silos. What are your thoughts on this as someone who uses digital culture to bring people together around African literature?

**Ainehi Edoro:** I think there are two types of social media. There is the social media or the web culture of the 1990s, when people like Tim Berners-Lee and Harold Rheingold were trying to formulate what this new communication technology was. There was something very beautifully utopian about that moment. Rheingold imagined the 'virtual community' in which people could do so much while they're nonetheless separated by distance. They couldn't kiss each other. They couldn't punch each other. But they could still connect and do things socially that are meaningful. People were also thinking about the web as a kind of information architecture, this Foucauldian utopia where we could suddenly create knowledge, manage knowledge, distribute knowledge virtually, all in these grand databases. The idea was to use the web as a way both to connect people and to create knowledge.

Then something happened in the mid-2000s. This new moment begins with Facebook. Suddenly these companies realize that this idea of information architecture and virtual community could become the basis of these grand, rapacious, capitalistic structures. You could monetize this thing that started out in the dream of getting people together and creating knowledge. I think it's important to make that distinction between when the web was simply about distributing knowledge and getting people together, on the one hand, and the moment it shifted into something different, on the other hand. This moment was something that brought in the financial, commercial, capitalistic aspects of the web in its most diabolical form. I'm not blind to the ways in which web culture, especially as it emerges within social media, is highly problematic. It's shifting our worlds in ways that even Facebook cannot anticipate what the true threat is.

Notwithstanding that though, there are aspects of this technology that are incredibly interesting in how it allows us to create knowledge and constitute communities and discourses. For somebody like myself who works in African literature, and who has seen first-hand how knowledge and power can be used to erase and silence genealogies, I want to hold onto the utopian possibilities in social media as this thing that can allow us to right the wrongs of history; to make sure that Africa is at the centre of whatever kinds of discursive regimes are going to come out of social media. In my work – in *Brittle Paper* – I'm always thinking deeply about how I can use social media methodologically. How can I think about it in ways that allow me to create knowledge and understand how the archive works, so that in eighty years' time we're not still mourning the African past like we're doing right now?

**Joel Cabrita:** Thinking more specifically about this issue of knowledge production and the work that a platform like *Brittle Paper* does, of all our interlocuters, you are the sole figure who works purely in the world of online literature. So, do you think of yourself as a publisher? Do you consider yourself doing the same thing that colleagues like Bibi Bakare-Yusuf is doing with Cassava Press or Lousie Umutoni is doing with Huza Press, but just doing those things online?

**Ainehi Edoro:** I am an online publisher. Yesterday, I had a call with Colleen Higgs. She runs Modjaji Books out of Cape Town and is putting together a catalogue for small publishers on the continent. It's an amazing project. She's essentially trying to create a space where publishers across the continent can talk to each other. I asked her, 'Do you have a space for online publications?' and she was like, 'Well, I guess I should think about that.' In a sense, Colleen doesn't see us online publishers as publishers in the print culture definition of what publishing is. I completely understand where she's coming from. I think it's actually healthy to maintain that distinction because what we do is different from print publishers. They exist within a different circulation economy than I do. What I do is to put things in circulation, but the kinds of things I place in circulation, and how I do it, are different. You know, they – physical publishers – have these very specific institutional frameworks that define the way that the books are circulated. I am interested not so much in books, but in the ways that a tweet is a tool of circulation in the same way that a book is.

What is a book? A book is not anything magical. A book is essentially a receptacle that makes the transfer of information cheap and easy, right? It's like an album. It's a very cheap way to gather together its own information and move it from place to place. What is a tweet? A tweet is essentially the same thing, which is a way to take a fragment of information moving from place to place and make it visible and allow people to have access to it. It's stored. It's archived just like a book.

For me, publishing exists within that world where I am concerned with circulation – simply getting people to see things. I am concerned about the ways in which that type of circulation allows you to constitute communities, but also to create discourses: to essentially have this space where you can change the narrative. You can direct the way people ask questions. You can change the vectors of conversations. And you can do it with very limited resources. Again, for someone who works within the African archives where we have had issues with the fact that people control what can be said or not said about our worlds, it's incredibly important to me that I exist in a space where I can contribute by controlling or influencing the ways that discussions are generated around cultural objects that I care about.

**Joel Cabrita:** The dual function of *Brittle Paper* seems to be both an online platform for publishing new work by authors but also to act as a kind of online magazine. You're both commenting on literary culture as well as publishing literature. That resonates with what you were saying about this ability of spaces like *Brittle Paper* to shape the conversation. This is a way in which you seem quite distinct from a traditional publisher – you have this curated section of literary industry news and happenings alongside the creative work that you're publishing.

**Ainehi Edoro:** Yeah. That's a good way to think about the kind of content that *Brittle Paper* creates. We publish original stuff, but we're mainly known for the kind of curatorial work we do for the literary scene. It's great to publish novels and publish books, but I think that books – as the cultural object that defines a literary scene – are just one part of the whole. There's a ton of work that involves creating discourse around books. That is what scholars are paid to do: to look at an archive and then create discourses around it and ensure that we use the archive to transmit knowledge over time. If we don't do this, then an archive is just a collection of books that sit there. *Brittle Paper* is doing something similar. When something happens, we say it has happened. And when we say it has happened, people are able to respond to it. That's why the news content – the news aggregation aspects of *Brittle Paper* – is very important to me. It is one of the fun parts of the project. What has been special over the years is figuring out what this commentary is. What kind of curating are we doing? What things are we bringing in the mix? What things are we leaving out?

When we started out – when I decided that this site was going to be an African literature-centred site – I wanted to feature news content. Who is publishing what? Who is signing what deal? Who is on what shortlists? To be a place where you can come for news about African literature as a global construct. Then I realized that in addition to what's considered 'literary news', there are all these other peripheral kinds of information that authors generate about their lives that don't quite fit into the classic literary text or the biographical authorial text. When Chimamanda Adichie has an Instagram account where she is essentially sharing her love for fashion and style, what do I do with that? Or when Emmanuel Iduma and Ayobami Adebayo go on Instagram and over one week each of them writes these beautiful affirmations of love to each other. These are two amazing African writers that we never knew were dating and then one day they come on Instagram and say, 'Oh yeah, we're not just in love, we are married and we're going to spend four days writing absolutely gorgeous captions professing our love to each other.' What do I do with that information? Or like when Nnedi Okorafor introduces us to her cat, Periwinkle Chukwu, who has a Twitter account and talks like a cat in the Twitter account, or when Okey Ndibe has this amazing love story with his wife that he has been with for decades. What do you do with those kinds of content that don't really fit anywhere? I felt like, 'Okay, maybe *Brittle Paper* could be the space where we're talking about hardcore literary news, but we're also making space for this extra-literary thing that I think completes the story of what a literary community is.' It might not be literary to look at wedding pictures, but it adds intimacy to what it means to imagine an African literary community.

**Joel Cabrita:** It seems to me that you're redefining what literature is and challenging us to rethink of our characterization of these other parts of literary culture – love, romance, fashion, pets – as ephemeral. You're moving these elements to the heart of the narrative about what literature is and how it's produced, rather than insignificant fripperies. A different topic now. Please talk to us about money. You mentioned that publishing can be done cheaper as an online platform, but how do you do it? How is revenue generated by an online platform like *Brittle Paper*?

**Ainehi Edoro:** There are different phases to the project. I'll talk about it in terms of how the project has grown over the years. It started out as a blog I was writing in grad school. At this point, it just required web-hosting costs and my time. So it's possible to start out projects like this in a very simple way and I recommend starting things out that way. If you can get a ton of funding to launch an online platform, then good. But, if you don't, just start out very small and it doesn't take anything to be able to launch a project. Web hosting fees are minimal. If you're in a university, you can also get free access to technology. As things go on, they get slightly more expensive because when a digital content creation site begins to grow, you need more content. That's the thing, web culture is this voracious insatiable beast. In the Nigerian fantasist, Amos Tutuola's novel *The Palm Wine Drinkard*, there is something called the hungry creature. When I think about web culture, especially social media, I think the hungry creature is a perfect metaphor for it. It is this creature that tells you it's hungry. It keeps crying, 'I'm hungry, I'm hungry, I'm hungry'. You give it something. It eats it and continues crying, 'I'm hungry, I'm hungry, I'm hungry'. It eats everything around it. It will eat your bag. At some point, it will eat you. That's what I think of web culture. So the bigger you grow, the more you need content and I think that was the first cost I incurred. It was paying for somebody to join the team and produce content with me. The team has grown since then and much of my funding goes towards personnel – towards getting people to create content. I could still use more people.

The other thing where cost is incurred is with the graduate complexity of the technology. As a project begins to grow and become more complicated – and as you become more creative in terms of what you think can be done – you realize that technology now costs money. It is no longer your free WordPress site that you started out with. We did a website redesign last year and included certain new functionalities like a database of African books just to help us handle our curation work. We create tonnes of book lists throughout the year and two major lists – the anticipated list of the year and the notable books list at the end of the year. We realized that we can optimize that technologically in a way that serves us now and also in the future. It costs money. But it's not cheap and things break. I would say that the key things that we need money for are technology and personnel.

I started very conservatively. I never wait till I have figured out everything before I jump in and the only way I can do that is by starting small. I tried to keep costs to a minimum. For a long time, *Brittle Paper* was funded from my personal income, but now I've been able to get some support from the University of Wisconsin-Madison and Google ads. We are also trying to figure out a way to create products and services that we can sell and make money from. The reason why we're trying to be as financially sustainable as we can is because we've seen situations where African cultural platforms get a tonne of funding from funding sources, but when the funding stops, the organization can't survive. I don't want that to happen to *Brittle Paper*. When you rely solely on external funding, it shifts the kind of work that you do. That's why starting out I always wanted *Brittle Paper* to run on a profit model to force us to actually think creatively about organically sustaining the system.

**Michelle Julia Ng:** Changing gears from this topic, could you reflect on how you think about language? You've obviously taken the decision to use English as the primary language for *Brittle Paper*. How do you position yourself in the debate about whether English is an African language?

**Ainehi Edoro:** This is a very old, old, old conversation and it has been staged in all kinds of different ways. The place of English in African literary discourse raises for me the problem of investment. I agree with Ngũgĩ wa Thiong'o that we just do not invest enough in African languages, at least, not as much as we do in these other languages. So I want to think about the issue in those terms of investment, not in terms of whether one position is politically weird or shady and the other position is right. We have invested a lot in English and in its institutions, and this is also true for the way that English exists in African countries and constitutes the discourse of those worlds. But we've just not done the same with African languages. To me, that is the problem. With a space like *Brittle Paper*, I get a ton of inquiry on African languages. Why don't you have an African language section? To be honest, it would take a lot for me to create a section where you can have content in Zulu or Yoruba or Hausa. It would be terribly difficult to do. English is just very convenient. But that's the kind of attitude we need to critique, right? There are ways in which we could invest in African languages by creating spaces for its expression, its visibility, allowing it to generate knowledge for us. Digital technology has actually given us affordable tools to do that. So why aren't we doing that? For me, that would be the question as opposed to asking whether it's bad for us to think in English or work in English. At what point are we going to shape up and really invest in these languages?

**Olayinka Adekola:** We've thought a bit about the practice of archiving African literature – Bibi Bakare-Yusuf also makes a lot of that notion. Do you think your mandate as a publisher is to create an archive of African stories?

**Ainehi Edoro:** Ola, that's a very good question, because it allows us to think about archives in different ways. For Bibi as a publisher, she's essentially creating the primary cultural objects that we have in the archive. Let's make it clear that we're thinking about the archive not just as actual objects that exist in the canon or on the bookshelf. We're thinking about archives also in the way that Jacques Derrida might think about it. Archives are the ways in which we set up rules that tell us what to put on the bookshelves or not to, or what we can or cannot say about the things we have on the bookshelf. The archive is both the thing and the rules that govern the way we talk about the thing, and the way we allow ourselves to imagine it as something that exists in the world. African literature as an archive is the actual novels and the books, but it's also the ways in which we decide how we're going to talk about African literature, and how we're going to allow African literature as a thing to exist in the world and be transmittable across time.

Bibi and Ellah Wakatama and all these amazing women – by the way, most of them are women – are doing an amazing job in trying to create all kinds of different cultural literary objects that constitute the African literary archive. But I think that there is another work that also needs to be done, in terms of archiving the things that we are saying about these objects, recording what we are allowed to say at a particular moment in time about these objects. When Bibi talks about the archive as being of the future, that's precisely what she's saying. In eighty years' time when we come back and look at this moment, we can see the limits and possibilities in the ways that we talked about what constitutes African literature.

For me, *Brittle Paper* and similar spaces are precisely in that zone, where we are archiving the ways that we are talking about the novel. We are archiving the chatter, the conversation, the discussion that is being had around the novel. I was just thinking the other day that if I wanted to know what Wole Soyinka thought about the process of writing a novel, I won't even know where to start. I would have to go into the library and dig and look for interviews that are out of print. It would be so laborious. But today it's easy to figure out what authors think about their work, what they think about culture, what they think about the archive, because there are spaces like *Brittle Paper* collecting these conversations, this chatter that everybody is having and gathering it in a place where they are durable and where they can be transmitted through time. To me, that is what an archive is.

**Joel Cabrita:** I certainly see the appeal of having this all curated in the same site that also presents you with the author's work, that the conversation around the work is folded into the work itself. What also strikes me as interesting is that you use words like durable and enduring. Previously you mentioned the fleeting or fragile aspects of online publishing. But nothing is ever truly 'lost' on the internet whereas things are lost all the time in paper archives.

**Ainehi Edoro:** There's an interesting tension. We do think of the digital space as being ephemeral or fragile. I see what we do at *Brittle Paper* and similar spaces as kinds of rescue projects. When somebody says something on Twitter, it will disappear. But what if we rescue it and publish it on *Brittle Paper* and it's there for people to see in fifteen years' time? There's a redemptive process involved in digital content creation, in the sense that you are making sure things don't get lost. Shailja Patel wrote this amazing fourteen-tweet thread critiquing Adichie's flippant response to postcolonial theory. Those tweets are the best commentary on feminism and capitalism and postcolonial literature that I've ever seen, but they could have just been lost. But they are there on *Brittle Paper* until today. It's been one of our most successful posts ever, it's garnered over 200,000 hits. That work of rescuing things from the heap of social media so that we can have it to transmit – that's also part of what is involved in the curatorial work that we do.

**Kyle Wang:** You touched on this earlier when discussing the early years of the internet and the potential it seemed to hold not only for creating new forms of knowledge production but for making new communities. In today's social media landscape, how do you think there's space to reimagine how literary communities can form? For example, can things like writers' conferences be reimagined for exclusively online spaces?

**Ainehi Edoro:** I don't think they can. It's something that I've had the opportunity to observe because of the Covid pandemic. Online spaces are great for interactions that allow us to create content. If you compare Black Lives Matter protests and the civil rights marches of the 1960s, what's different about them is that the civil rights protesters didn't have phones to take pictures with and then tweet with. You went on a march, but you couldn't really generate content around the march. But with the Black Lives Matter protests, there was a protest, but there was also this massive creation of media content around it. So online spaces connect us within the context of creating media content around something. When I post something on Instagram and Leila Aboulela comments on it, we are connecting, but she has also commented and left a kind of media footprint. I think digital spaces are amazing for things like that – creating communities through the generation of content. That's what Facebook essentially is; you connect people based on what they say about their world and their lives.

But life cannot be reduced to content, right? That's why we need real-life spaces where we can all meet and we can all talk.

When I go to the Ake festival, it's not just about the panels. The panels are 20 per cent of what the festival is. The festival is also about the affective power of meeting bodies, touching people, hugging people, falling in love, fighting with people, meeting publishers. There's something electrifying about occupying space with our bodies. That's why I think in a situation where you do an entire conference and all you have are video footages and comments, that is reducing life to the media objects we can create about life. While that is good, it can certainly not be the only way that we interact with each other. We need our bodies to occupy space.

**Joel Cabrita:** Earlier you mentioned that women currently dominate the African publishing scene. I read an interview with you from 2017 where you stated that 'African literature is a girls' club at the moment'. Talk to us more about gender. Women writers are everywhere and many key publishing figures on the continent are women. Why is this happening, particularly when we think of the historic domination of African literature by men? And as an adjacent question, how helpful do you think it is to think in terms of male writers, women writers, male publishers, female publishers, while trying to have a greater sensitivity to issues of gender fluidity? Are these outmoded categories, and is using binary gender constructions the most productive way forward?

**Ainehi Edoro:** I would say that what has changed is digital technology. That's really the only thing I can imagine that is different about where we were before and where we are now. There's something about print culture that seems like it lends itself to a certain type of masculine way of constituting power.

Maybe it has to do with the very rigidly hierarchical nature of both print technology and the culture around it. We know that women are doing much better in terms of social media influencer culture than men are doing, right? There's something about digital technology that feeds into a certain way that femininity has been constructed. I'm just riffing here... There's a kind of specularity to social media, it's very much about the body, about being visible.

So yes, women are the ones publishing all the novels that are making waves and women are the ones involved in institutional spaces. If you think about Lola Shoneyin with Ake festival, she singlehandedly changed the way that festivals work on the continent. When you think about what we are doing at *Brittle Paper*, it seems that these spaces are very much being occupied by women right now, and of course that's a shift from the world in which men dominated. I'm not complaining! Of course, we are going to have to think deeply about what the cause is, or what the implications are, but I certainly see it as a welcome development.

In terms of thinking about culture through gender binaries, I do think they don't necessarily tell the full story. But I defer to Mona Eltahawy's book *Seven Necessary Sins for Women and Girls*, in which she wants to tie up feminism with dismantling gender binaries. We have to think about a kind of feminism that allows us to also think about queer trans experiences. Recently I watched a Zoom conversation on radical African feminism and all the panellists agreed that we have to think about gender in ways that dismantle the binary. The fact that women are beginning to find their place in African literary production is also a signal that this is a space that is beginning to open up toward queer experiences and trans experiences.

For a long time, African literature has been really vicious about erasing queer experiences. There was literally no space to think about queer life except as something inauthentic or something problematic. But things are changing. We are seeing an African literary space in which queer voices are being unsilenced – what Akwaeke Emezi is doing with trans experiences is amazing. It's all part of a broader move away from a culture dominated by the ideals of a masculine culture.

**Joel Cabrita:** When Louise Umutoni visited with us, she was a week away from having a baby (see conversation on page 113). There's no way that in the physical world a woman on the verge of giving birth could be engaged in a conversation thousands of miles away from her home. Online engagement seems to redefine reproductive labour, meaning it's no longer an impediment to a woman's ability to be intellectually active and engaged.

**Ainehi Edoro:** When I was pregnant, I kept giving talks all through my pregnancy. I looked a little different on my videos, but I was able to keep working. We don't think about how this seemingly small structural change is part of what it means to redefine the world in ways that take feminist thought into account. Thinking about queer experiences, there's perhaps a way that digital culture has made it more possible, because it makes it easier to make space. I remember in the early days at *Brittle Paper,* I received this amazing poem from a writer who said he had sent it to other places, and he was told point blank that 'we don't publish work about gay experiences'. And so he sent it to us. Of course, we were happy to publish it. And now you're seeing digital spaces – Facebook conversation,

Instagram accounts, websites, even online magazines – giving voice to queer writers in ways that traditional publishing would have silenced or erased. Digital culture is making the discursive space more diverse, richer, more textured.

**Michelle Julia Ng:** In an ideal world, where would you take *Brittle Paper*? What's your long-term dream?

**Ainehi Edoro:** My long-term vision for *Brittle Paper* is to seek out other ways that it can impact culture. Digital content creation is very important, but I would also like to do other kinds of capacity-building. We receive ton of submissions from young writers on the continent who struggle with skill and craft development. In part, it's because they just don't have access to affordable training platforms. I would love to have training platforms for writers. I would also love to design a *Brittle Paper* festival celebrating online writing, corralling writers globally who produce work in the digital space and have us all think about what it means to work on African literature in the digital sphere. I would also like to expand into some kind of publishing platform, one that gives space to very quirky, weird literary texts that typically would not make their way through the normal publishing channels. I think of *Brittle Paper* as a brand that could expand into all these other cultural spheres, but the goal will always be to keep expanding African literature – to keep expanding its impact and to maintain its footprint in the digital sphere.

**About Ainehi Edoro:** Ainehi is an assistant professor of English at the University of Wisconsin-Madison, where she teaches and researches in African literature, political theory, and literature in social media. Ainehi is also the founder and editor of *Brittle Paper*, a leading online platform for African writing and literary culture. She writes essays and commentaries about contemporary African literary culture in publications like *The Guardian* and *Africa is a Country*.

*'What we wanted to do from the
very start was to produce and disseminate
African stories, told from an
African perspective.'*

# IN CONVERSATION WITH:
# LOUISE UMUTONI

20 January 2021

**Olayinka Adekola and Barry Migott:** Could you tell us more about the history of how you started Huza Press and the steps that took you there?

**Louise Umutoni:** I started Huza Press in 2015. To be honest, it wasn't something that I had set out to do. I was simply very passionate about African voices. I also wanted to add my voice to that small but growing African literary archive. Ever since I can remember, I wanted to produce and consume African content in books and magazines. However, like many of my peers, I had to settle for mostly Western literature even if a lot of the experiences encountered in these books felt foreign. Don't get me wrong, I enjoyed reading the stories and there is something about the human experience that makes it universal. It's just the context in which these stories were set that seemed so removed from my own experiences.

It wasn't until I was about twelve that I read my first African novel. It was *The Concubine* by Elechi Amadi and I was hooked. I spent hours in libraries looking for similar books. It was how I first encountered Ngũgĩ, Achebe and Ayi Kwei Armah. The initial excitement was short-lived as I quickly realized that there wasn't a lot of African literature available. At the time I started Huza Press in 2015, it was clear that this was quickly changing. I was increasingly aware that there was this movement across the continent and the proliferation of literary works from contemporary African writers. It entailed a pushback against the idea that the only African literature worth its name was from the 1960s to the 1980s.

We were being introduced to new voices like Chimamanda Adichie, NoViolet Bulawayo, Binyavanga Wainaina and others. Our stories were being discussed in mainstream media and there was a growing interest in African literary works. Around that time, I started to research what was happening in the literary space in Rwanda. I was surprised to find that this wave had barely touched Rwanda. This movement that was so prominent in places like Kenya and Nigeria was largely missing in Rwanda. The publishing space was completely dominated by the schoolbook market and the shelves of the handful of bookshops in Kigali were filled with Western titles. The reading culture was also still poor compared to Rwanda's neighbours. So I thought, this is what I want to change. It was a mammoth task. At the time, I did not realize how hard or how long it would take to see progress. It was in that context that Huza Press was born.

**Olayinka Adekola and Barry Migott:** So if your goal has been to promote African knowledge production and dissemination, what does Huza Press consider to be African writing? Who do you consider an African writer? Must they be based in Africa?

**Louise Umutoni:** This is something that I've been asked before. I will start by saying that I'm not a huge fan of putting work by African writers under the African literature tag in bookshops. There are lots of things about that [approach] that are not very exciting, the most important being that it is quite limiting. Some people do want to be identified as African writers. I can't remember if it was Taiye Selasi who said that – don't quote me on this one – but why label it as African writing? Why not base it on the theme, or the genre, as opposed to who is writing it? You don't see a lot of other books from across the world identified with the origin of the writer. Beyond this issue of where it's placed in a bookshop, when I think of an African writer or African writing, I think of work that's created by someone from the continent. They could be residing on the continent or not, it doesn't really matter to me. It's somebody who has roots on the continent and that is informing their writing.

**Olayinka Adekola and Barry Migott:** Thanks for that, Louise. Can you talk us through some of the logistical issues you encountered in setting up Huza? How did you actually get things going and how did you structure it in the early days?

**Louise Umutoni:** At first, I thought Huza would be a nonprofit. And I remember one of the first people I spoke to about this was Kate Wallis who is currently the co-director of Huza Press. She put me in touch with Ellah Wakatama who had been working in the industry for a very long time. I remember Ellah saying to me, 'Well, Louise, listen, you've got to promise me this is not going to be a nonprofit. You've got to make sure that it operates like a proper business. So you do not do what's been done historically, which is deprive the African book of its value, by not selling it at its value.' Devaluing of the African book has been going on for decades with NGOs or non-profits commissioning the production of certain works and then distributing the books produced from that process for free. This process has stifled the growth of the publishing industry by distorting the incentive structures around book production and dissemination. It has discouraged the creation of publishing infrastructure on the continent as the books are produced elsewhere and since quality isn't emphasized there is no work done to build the expertise required to produce good quality books. So at the time, I immediately thought, 'Well, it's going to be a business.' I took Ellah's advice. I was able to get some funding through a business accelerator programme to put together a small team of two at the time. We decided that we were going to run a new prize for fiction to try and understand what was actually being written about in Rwanda. Like I said, there was just nothing that was being produced in Rwanda that was not for the schoolbook market. We ran our first literary prize as a publishing house and we were just blown away by how much we received, blown away by the range of stories that people were sending in, the fact that people were writing about all kinds of things. At first, we thought most of the submissions would be on the genocide as that was the dominant theme in the writing on Rwanda. Don't get me wrong, there is nothing wrong with writing on the genocide in Rwanda as that is an important part of our story. But we wondered if there would be other themes, and we were pleasantly surprised that this was the case. People were writing about love, about marriage, sci-fi, friendship and more. We started to get a sense of what was out there. But we also got a sense of some of the gaps, particularly around writing. Some of the basic concepts on what constitutes a story were lacking in a lot of the work. This revealed gaps in the education system, including challenges with language of instruction. Rwanda over the years switched the language of instruction in schools from French to English and you could clearly see the impact of this in some of the submissions where there wasn't a good grasp of the language being used. We started to explore the value of working in the three languages used in Rwanda, including Kinyarwanda. We also felt the need for some more targeted training around creative writing and how to put together a narrative properly. We then started a mentorship scheme, where we paired every shortlisted writer with an established African writer. Some amazing people worked with us, people like Jennifer Nansubuga Makumbi, Taiye Selasi, Shadreck Chikoti and Richard Ali. Really amazing African authors volunteered to support the Rwandan writers that were just starting out. We were able to publish our first anthology from that *Versus and Other Stories.* We've since published many other titles and worked with amazing authors from across the continent. We've also done quite a lot of capacity building, whether in the creative writing space or in the editorial space. We've tried to build the ecosystem that would support our work because it was very clear that we needed to do that.

**Olayinka Adekola and Barry Migott:** Could you be more specific about what that Rwandan literary ecosystem looked like and what was lacking?

**Louise Umutoni:** We had to do capacity building in most of the skills that we needed to produce books, including editing, proofreading, cover design and typesetting. This work is still ongoing but I think we're starting to see some gains. For example, we now don't have to go beyond Rwanda to find a cover designer. We know that we have people that can do that here. Also, we've seen some amazing Rwandan writers publishing their work beyond Rwanda and being included in the Caine Prize anthology.[1] We supported Rwandan writers to submit their stories to the Caine Prize and we hosted the Caine Prize workshop in Rwanda for the first time [in 2018]. Seeing all these wonderful Rwandan stories find space in established journals and literary magazines has been very important for us at Huza. Beyond our work in Rwanda, we've also worked with writers from other parts of the continent, like Billy Kahora and many others.

**Olayinka Adekola and Barry Migott:** So further along these lines, what do you consider the scope of your publishing house to be? Do you think of yourself as a Rwandan press, an African press, or an international press?

**Louise Umutoni:** We think of ourselves as all those things. You could say we are an African publisher because we don't only publish Rwandan writing, we publish work by writers from across the continent. We would say that we are an African publishing house because we are interested in African content, and we're interested in telling African stories.

---

[1]   The stories written at Caine Prize workshops are published annually alongside the Prize's shortlisted stories in anthology form. http://www.caineprize.com/anthologies.

**Olayinka Adekola and Barry Migott:** You've spoken about some of the challenges – as well as strides forward – in terms of literary capacity building. Thinking more specifically about your own local context, what are some of the other major challenges in running a publishing house in Rwanda?

**Louise Umutoni:** Running a publishing house in Rwanda is probably just as difficult as running a publishing house anywhere else on the continent. One shared challenge is distribution. Distribution has been our biggest issue on the continent for years. We have linkages to the West, but not linkages with each other on the continent. It's much easier for me to get my books to London than it is to get my books to Nigeria or Ghana. It's really hard because the distribution links haven't been properly established. So as publishers within the continent, we are currently having discussions with each other to try and address some of these things. The infrastructure is just not there. The trade links are not properly established. We have to go against this tide. It's one of those issues which are far more difficult to address without support from governments or support from some big players in the public and in the private sector.

The other big one is infrastructure around publishing, say for example, printing presses. We have to do our printing in India, and it's much better quality and cheaper [than printing locally]. This is the same for quite a lot of publishers on the continent. It's cheaper for me to print in India than it is for me to print in South Africa. That's problematic. So, that issue needs addressing. And do we have good proofreaders? Do we have good typesetters? Do we have good cover designers or illustrators? We don't have that many on the continent that are good and have built this expertise over time. And yes, we've had some training here and there, but it's not been as targeted. These kinds of literary infrastructure also haven't been around for that long. I know the African Writers Trust does some work around building editorial capacities.[2] Huza Press is also thinking about doing some coaching. We'd have an established editor working with an African editor on a particular text over a period of time and the two of them would produce this text together. That's something we have already started doing with some of our titles. But the gap is still huge and we have a big need for some really targeted interventions in that space. Without long-term support we won't be able to build a group of really good, say, editors across the continent.

Then there are issues of capital. You've got an industry that has not been around for long and there are questions around whether it's actually going to survive and the changes that have to be made for the African publishing industry to survive. It's not easy to access capital. You find that a lot of us are really struggling financially to keep our work going. A lot of our profits are quite small. And that means that we only have so much capacity to produce a few titles here and there every year. I would like to see some investment going into these spaces because, of course, production is always going to be important. One last issue, which is really particular to Rwanda, is around the culture of reading. And we've seen that it's grown over time, but it's never been that great historically. And I know this is

---

[2]  The African Writers Trust aims to bridge the divide between African writers and publishing professionals living in the Diaspora as well as on the continent. See here for their workshop programme: https://afri-canwriterstrust.org/category/professional-training-workshop-for-cre-ative-writers/.

something that's been actively debated on the continent and something that many find insulting but it's a perception that's held by many that if you want to hide something from an African, put it in a book. That's not completely fair. The reading culture in many African countries is great. I grew up in Uganda where street vendors would be seen reading newspapers. But it is also true that the reading culture could be better, especially here in Rwanda. There's been quite a lot of sensitization around getting children to read early on and to increase access so that we can create that culture of reading. We're not quite there yet.

**Olayinka Adekola and Barry Migott:** Talk to us about where you see your publishing company going in the future? In a dream world, with no limitations at all, what would it look like?

**Louise Umutoni:** That's always an interesting question. Probably like any other publishing business, our big goal would be to publish as many titles as we possibly can. I would like to be able to add to the African literary canon. I would love to have seen multiple African writers' voices added to that and for Huza Press to have been a fundamental part of that process. I'd also want for us to distribute beyond some of the existing geographical regions where we currently distribute. So we are currently exploring South America and Asia. Being able to reach those broader audiences is something that we are really keen on.

Also, to somehow find a way to sort out the distribution problem here in Africa. African titles tend not to travel as well across the continent. Which is sad because what we are doing is producing these titles, to be honest, primarily for the African reader, the African audience. But you don't get as much travelling of these books across the continent because distribution channels are not effective, they're not well established. And so you're limited to certain geographical areas, mostly cities.

**Olayinka Adekola and Barry Migott:** We're thinking extensively about the preferred languages of the various African publishers we are in conversation with. Of course, there's a very long-standing debate about the status of English in Africa as a corollary of colonization. What are your thoughts on this for your work with Huza Press? Do you see English and other European languages as African languages?

**Louise Umutoni:** I'd very quickly say that I don't think English is an African language. But there have been instances where the English language has been reshaped and bent to the needs and demands of those peoples that were forced to use it. For example, Pidgin in Nigeria, and Sheng in Kenya. I suppose this could be seen as a means to Africanize these foreign languages and probably reclaim a degree of agency in how they use them.

What is really interesting is the debate on whether European languages should be used in African literature. That's one of the questions that has plagued the African publishing industry for some time now. It's recently been popularized by Ngũgĩ [wa Thiong'o] who has championed more writing in African languages and comes against the more practical issue of access. So unfortunately, European languages such as English and French have been used across the continent in such a way that they do allow for accessibility across different borders and across different languages and ethnicities.

As a publisher, I tend to lean towards the more practical

position that publishing in English or French seems to work better in terms of access. And what we are concerned with at Huza Press is access, such that the work we are producing is able to transcend our borders. In Rwanda we are quite lucky that we actually have one language that we all speak – Kinyarwanda. It's not the same with other countries. In Uganda for example, which is right next door to us, you have more than fifty languages. In Rwanda we've made a conscious decision to publish more work in Kinyarwanda if the content is by a Rwandan author for example. But we'd also use Kinyarwanda if we feel it's the sort of content that would work quite well for the Rwandan audience. But I'm not going to lie and say that it's practical to completely discard English as a publishing language. Because this is a language that has gained a foothold in our countries and is far reaching. It allows us to ensure that our stories go beyond our own borders and speak to a broader audience. And as a publisher we are hoping to sell to a broader audience. The numbers matter from a practical stance. I'm sure that there are people who have different opinions about this language issue. I know, for example, Nigerian authors and Nigerian publishers who are quite lucky to be in a position whereby they've got massive audiences for Hausa, for example, or Yoruba. We don't have the same with Kinyarwanda. Even if we're talking about the whole of Rwanda, it's still quite a small population that buys books and would not make business sense to limit our sales to that very small audience.

But I think it's much broader than just a business question. It's also an issue of access. It's also an issue of our stories getting to different audiences. Of course, speaking to ourselves is important. But we also want to speak to others. And that's one mission that's been at the core of Huza Press. What we wanted to do from the very start was to produce and disseminate African stories, told from an African perspective. So that's not possible if we're restricting it by language and just publishing purely in Kinyarwanda, or Luganda if we're publishing a Ugandan book. That's my stance on this. Of course, it doesn't mean that it's resolved on my end. I still struggle with it as well. And I would much rather we were in a different position, but that's the way things are.

**Olayinka Adekola and Barry Migott:** So thinking in very practical and concrete terms, how exactly do you determine which language to use for publication of a particular book?

**Louise Umutoni:** From our end, it's about who we are trying to reach with a particular title. That's the most important question. If our primary audience for the title is, say, in Rwanda, then, you know, we're primarily going to publish in Kinyarwanda and really push that language of publication for that title. If we think that there could be a much wider audience for that title, for example, an audience more in the Anglophone space, then we will publish that title in English. We can also do the same for titles that we think will have wider readership in the Francophone world. What I find is most useful for us, because we work across multiple languages, is to think through whether a title could actually reach multiple audiences.

If we know that it's a really good one, then we will publish it in multiple languages. As I mentioned before, our core mission is to insert African voices into the existing canon on Africa or the existing knowledge on Africa. So we've got to be able to publish in a language that is going to reach as wide an audience as possible. We'd have a title in English to start with and then it would be translated. Translation is a huge part of what we do. We try to ensure that a lot of our titles are translated or if we find a title that's been published and we feel strongly about the story and want to expand its reach then we do consider translating it. That's what we did with Yolande Mukagasana's *Not My Time to Die*, which had previously been published in French.

**Olayinka Adekola and Barry Migott:** We'd like to shift gears for a moment, to think about an issue that's particularly close to our own hearts and about which we're curious to hear your thoughts. In terms of reaching as many different people as possible, the multiple audiences you mentioned above, what work do you do in terms of starting new conversations about sexuality? Even though LGBTQ+ issues are considered taboo across much of the African continent, do you see this as part of your mission in terms of giving African LGBTQ+ authors a voice?

**Louise Umutoni:** You're right that these are taboo issues in many parts across the continent. I mean, right next door in Uganda, there is an [anti-]homosexuality law and it's not exactly the most conducive space for LGBTQ+ voices. It's quite complex to address these issues on the continent. On our end, we've actually worked with some authors addressing these issues and our role is to provide a space for these stories to be told. However, it's still difficult to find a lot of writers willing to write about this. And of course, it's not their fault. It's not the most welcoming culture [for LGBTQ+ individuals]. Here in Rwanda, for example, there's no specific law against it, but it's also not a very welcoming culture in general towards people of that community. So it makes it very complex.

What we can do is ensure that it is very clear that our platform is very open and available to people writing about these issues. And that they are aware that we will support them because, of course, like I said, it's really important that these marginalized voices – particularly those from the continent talking about issues that have been primarily talked about by the West – are allowed a platform to be able to tell their side of the story or just give their perspectives on what it means for them. Across the continent, we could do with more voices on these issues because what's resulted from this silence is a lot of misconceptions about how sexuality and LGBTQ+ issues are perceived in Africa. What you see from a lot of Western perspectives on this issue is that African societies are completely averse to discussing alternative sexualities. It's more complex than that. These are societies that are not necessarily averse but are talking about these issues in different ways and in different spaces. Allowing those voices into mainstream narratives is really important.

**Olayinka Adekola and Barry Migott:** So summing up this conversation, how do you feel your work has had an impact on people's lives? And how do you measure success?

**Louise Umutoni:** As I've mentioned, the primary driver for the work that we do is to provide space for voices from the continent to speak about their own experiences, from their own perspectives, and to get that inserted into the existing narrative about African lives and experiences. So for me the way that I measure success is through asking how many writers we have allowed access to our platforms, how many writers' voices we have been able to augment, how many African writers' voices we have inserted into the African literary canon.

And in terms of how I feel that work has impacted people's lives… it's really hard to measure whether people's perspectives on other people's experiences have changed. I think what you can measure is whether you have a multiplicity of voices on a particular issue. Most importantly, it's not just the outsiders' gaze and interpretation of your experiences that is the dominant voice. What has always been a problem – and I've talked about this a couple of times – is that we have a continent that has struggled with the fact that the mainstream narrative about us and our experiences is not necessarily informed by us. As a result, it's not exactly the most accurate representation. What you have is someone else who has been telling stories about you for very many years. This has informed the mainstream perspective about who you are, and in some ways, you have people – especially young people – who are growing up reading about their experiences from other contexts, starting to see those interpretations of their context as the accurate interpretation. You know, that's not right.

So if there is anything that I would say I would have liked to have transformed or changed, it's to have added voices of those people from those contexts that had previously been written about by others. Saying, look, this is who I am. This is my experience. This is what it's like. That is very important. There's a sense of humanization. I would like to see that humanity being handed back to those people, because they're being made to feel that their voice is valued, their perspective is valued, their humanity is valued.

**About Louise Umutoni:** Louise Umutoni is the founder of Huza Press, a Rwandan-based publishing press devoted to supporting African literature. Huza Press has published writers such as Yolande Mukagasana, Billy Kahora and many emerging voices from across the continent. Huza Press also run one of the few prizes for fiction in Rwanda and launched some of the growing number of writers from Rwanda. Louise started her career as a journalist and worked as a regular reporter and contributor for several newspapers and magazines. She is passionate about knowledge creation and dissemination in Africa. She has also written academically on national liberation movements in Africa and women's political inclusion. Her work was selected for the Winihin-Jemide grant at the University of Oxford. In 2023, she started a PhD in African History at Yale University.

*'Institution-building is the act of reimagining and implementing new ways of doing necessary things, but with a focus on sustainability so that the impact is felt as widely as possible.'*

## IN CONVERSATION WITH:
## LOLA SHONEYIN

6 September 2021

**Joel Cabrita:** What's happening at the press and what's happening work-wise? What do your days look like at the moment?

**Lola Shoneyin:** It really depends on what time of the year it is. Right now, the first thing I attend to is the business of the Book Buzz Foundation, which translates to festival planning and preparation. I have a team of three young women. We discuss and debate ideas for the festival. We workshop our ideas for about an hour and a half, longer as the festival dates draw nearer. After this, I focus on the business of Ouida Books, the publishing house. Within our structure, there is a Managing Editor who works mainly on the flagship imprint. I still look after the other imprints, which comprises everything that's outside of core fiction. This means I work on the children's list, and our nonfiction list. I spend time with the editorial team so I put on my business hat. Sometimes, we edit and read manuscripts together. I do that for about two to three hours and then I turn to the other areas of the business. This includes the audio studio, the bookstore. It is really important to stay on top of book news so that we stock the books that people actually want to buy. I'm also opening a café so I am helping to develop the menu, the cuisine, the look and feel. Then, at the very end of the day, I do my own work which includes commissioned work, research, teaching and consulting. I try to get all my admin out of the way so I can go home with a clean conscience.

**Joel Cabrita:** When do you find time to write?

**Lola Shoneyin:** I find it difficult to engage the creative side of my brain during the working day. Having a young workforce means I have to be very hands-on. Any writing that I do, I do late at night, at home.

**Joel Cabrita:** How do you see this balance in identities between Lola as a writer and Lola as a businesswoman running this complex aggregate of publishing house, bookstore, foundation, festival, restaurant? Where do you feel the balance of power is lying right now, and are you happy with that balance?

**Lola Shoneyin:** I'm very happy with where I am because I don't see those different parts of me as being in competition or in conflict. Because my work is concentrated on the literary ecosystem, every aspect of Lola – the publisher, the festival organizer, the bookseller, the reader, the editor – all interact and have given me a deep and unique insight into that business. This is invaluable when I'm interacting with people from different areas of the publishing ecosystem. It's much easier to understand what's informing their decisions and actions.

**Joel Cabrita:** If you were to retrace the steps that led you to where you are today – this very multifaceted combination of professional identities where you're straddling very many things – how did this all begin? If you were telling the story of your life, what do you see as the major milestones you'd identify for the story?

**Lola Shoneyin:** I was very lucky. When I was about eight years old, I was at primary school in Edinburgh and the Prince of Wales came on a visit to the city. He'd just written a book – I still have my copy – called *The Old Man of Lochnagar.* So from very early on, I understood the relationship between the writer and the physical book. As a child, when I was reading, I would often wonder what the author was trying to tell me, like we had a secret pact. I started competing in poetry declamation contests when I was about nine years old at the Collegiate School in Bristol. Here I was trained to perform poetry and in reading clearly with meaning. Books and literature have always been part of my life. I was very lucky to have had an early introduction to the arts.

I was encouraged to read widely and write at the schools that I attended. I believed that this was everyone's experience. I started attempting to write long fiction in my teenage years. All my characters had English names because I was regurgitating the content of my literary diet at the time. You start with imitation, don't you? I never had a eureka moment when I decided that I wanted to be a writer but that changed when I got to Ogun State University, Nigeria. One of the lecturers pulled me aside and encouraged me to keep writing poetry and fiction. I enjoyed creative writing classes immensely and my lecturers would often single me out.

As soon as I left university, I joined the Association of Nigerian Authors [ANA]. I would go to the monthly readings and read my poems and my stories. I was a very committed member and at some point I was appointed as PR officer of the Oyo State chapter. I grew more confident and started entering my work for competitions. In one year I won both the prose prize and the poetry prize in Oyo State, which was very encouraging. Later in the same year, I entered my poetry manuscript for the ANA poetry national prize. My first collection of poems *So All the Time I Was Sitting on an Egg* made the shortlist. I was very elated. The two other poets on the shortlist were at least fifteen years older than I was.

I suppose I wanted to do more than write. So, at twenty-three years old, I founded a publishing house and named it Ovalonion House. I'd read Alice Walker and a few other books published by The Women's Press whose logo was an old-fashioned pressing iron. I also wanted to run an outfit that centred and promoted the work of women writers so our logo was an oval-shaped onion which looked like a womb. I was really interested in discovering talent so for a while I focused on editing poetry. On the side, I founded a literary pamphlet called *Olongo*. It was only sixteen pages long, so it was more like a newsletter. I would contact writers and encourage them to contribute poetry, stories and nonfiction. I couldn't afford to employ someone to do the layout so my husband taught me how to use Microsoft Publisher. I would then take the files to a printer in Mokola. I would watch them make the plates, roll, collate and staple.[1] I think spending time in the printing capital of Ibadan, surrounded by paper and books being bound and stitched, contributed to my fascination with book production.

I went back to university to get a postgraduate certificate in education, specializing in literature, media studies and drama. I taught in three inner-city London secondary schools. I'd done short stints in Nigerian schools before this. I would write, direct and produce plays for the school Christmas productions. My years as a teacher were some of my best. I learned so much from the system, my co-workers, my students, all of which is incredibly useful for the work that I do today.

I was twenty-five when I left Nigeria for the UK. I'd written two novels by that time, but I couldn't find a publisher. It was the year 2000 and it seemed that the mark of a successful African writer was having an international publisher. I was actively seeking West-facing agents and publishers. I was fresh out of the Iowa International Writing Program and I knew what the possibilities were. It was out of sheer exasperation that I started writing *The Secret Lives of Baba Segi's Wives*, which is the work that I'm best known for. I wrote it while I was in the UK, raising four children, in full-time education and then full-time work.

When I returned to Ibadan in the very early noughties, I founded the Ibadan Arts Renaissance, which was about music, art and writing, putting on shows and events that would bring people together to talk about and experience culture. At some point, I also opened a shop called Pata-Pata where I sold underwear.

[1]   Mokola is the printing capital of Ibadan, Oyo State, Nigeria.

**Joel Cabrita:** Why underwear?

**Lola Shoneyin:** I had a brainwave. I discovered that there were many middle-class [Nigerian] women like myself who only bought underwear in the UK. What if I brought the goods to them in Nigeria? A lot of the professional work hoovers up my personal resources so sometimes I have to think outside the 'Culture' box so that I can feed my family. I desperately needed a financially viable business venture.

**Joel Cabrita:** You used the phrase 'West facing' to refer to the sense that somehow you've made it if you've got a UK or international publisher. I'm interested to hear about the place of the UK in your personal cosmology. Given you've spent periods of time there, what does Britishness mean for you, both personally and as a publisher? I was very struck by the underwear story and the idea that the UK is the place you go to get those things. It feels like a lot of your work is trying to de-centre the UK and to make Nigeria an epicentre.

**Lola Shoneyin:** Marks and Spencer's underwear is something people of my age inherited from a generation of parents who went to university in the UK in the '60s. It became apparent to me quite quickly that I didn't have the confidence to 'build' in the UK. A lot of the structures were there already and I didn't feel connected to the environment. I think it has to do with the fact that I had schooled in the UK in the very early '80s, [a time] when people could be blatantly racist. Maybe I was slightly jaded. In any case, as soon as I touched down in Nigeria, I knew I was where I needed to be. People would call me 'Black Sambo' at school but the racial element didn't hit me until I saw the illustrations in *The Story of Little Black Sambo*. I was crushed that this was how people saw me. That's when it dawned on me, that I was different and that the 'N-word' wasn't just play. The realization that people treated me differently because of my skin colour made me fall out of love with everything I'd grown to love about the UK.

**Joel Cabrita:** These are such harrowing experiences for anyone, but especially for a young child. I'm so sorry to hear it. Thinking about your relationship to the UK now, with you running Ouida Books, what role does the UK play in your professional world?

**Lola Shoneyin:** Researching the history of publishing in Nigeria, you learn that a long list of British publishers had printing presses in Nigeria. There's no doubt that their presence helped accelerate the development of the Nigerian publishing scene. We had the population and the demand for schoolbooks, storybooks and research. Then one by one, most of them closed shop in the '80s during the military era – a sad period for intellectualism. However, in the last twenty years or so, the publishing industry has seen a renaissance, a reawakening of its past glory. Most of the new publishing houses are founded by Nigerians based in Nigeria. That's where I fit in. For me, the success of the UK publishing industry presents us with a case study. I am interested in studying what has worked, employing and adapting best practice for the Nigerian environment. I'm interested in building capacity and fostering a culture of excellence.

**Joel Cabrita:** Earlier you said that your first publishing house, which you amazingly founded at the age of twenty-three, was called Ovalonion, because that reminded you of the shape of a womb, and you were very inspired by women's publishers in the UK. Female empowerment seems like a theme for you.

**Lola Shoneyin:** Very much so. The opening section of my first collection of poems is called 'Clitoranguish'. I was reading up on a lot of African American feminist thought: Walker, Toni Cade Bambara, Ntozake Shange, Toni Morrison. I had a lot of confidence in my femininity. I probably have my upbringing to thank for that. I have five brothers and I've never been made to feel that there was something my brothers were doing that I couldn't do. My father made me believe that being a woman was not a barrier to accomplishment. Empowering women comes naturally to me.

**Joel Cabrita:** You previously described yourself as an 'institution-builder', and you've certainly built many institutions from presses to shops to festivals to a café. Tell me about your faith in institutions and where it comes from? Is institution -building a political act in a national context whereby certain state institutions are not being delivered upon?

**Lola Shoneyin:** When I was doing my dissertation at university, I couldn't find Toni Morrison's books in Nigeria. I had to get my brothers in the UK to buy them and send them to me. Access to knowledge has been greatly eroded and the state is not necessarily doing anything to re-energize and restore the institutions that people ordinarily go to in order to access knowledge. We're talking the libraries, we're talking bookstores, we're talking gatherings that feed the imagination and inspire you to think and do things differently. When I talk about institution-building, it's the act of taking deliberate steps to ensure that there is a strong foundation upon which viable structures can lean. When you help to create a demand for books, for instance, opportunities are created for other contributors within the ecosystem. In my case, I am interested in creating spaces where people can have serious conversations that challenge their thinking.

A few years ago, I visited South Africa for a festival. I met distinguished author Zakes Mda. He told me how the Black literary elite in South Africa sided with Biafra during Nigeria's Civil War because they had all read *Things Fall Apart*. It struck me in that moment that our conversations about decolonization and pan-Africanism were often stunted because of the lack of interaction between African countries. How can we identify and proffer long-standing solutions to the damage colonialism has done, if we don't know each other's stories, or have access to the ideas that inform our thinking? That's what inspired me to create OneRead – a mobile application that offers a different story from a different African country in Africa. It was about laying a foundation and introducing systems. And going back to this idea of institution-building, it's laying a foundation with a view to having concrete, long-term impact. It can be lonely, difficult work so it's important to stay focused and avoid distractions.

**Joel Cabrita:** Of course, one key institution is that of the actual physical printing presses. You mentioned the printers with whom you worked. Have you maintained these relationships?

**Lola Shoneyin:** Well, there's that idea that publishing is 'the office work' – the editing, the design, layout – the nice stuff that you can do from behind a desk. But when I have a curiosity, I do all the research that is available to me. I have no fear of going into unfamiliar spaces. I have spent hours in Shomolu, meeting printers, asking questions about paper, begging them to show me how things work.[2] Understanding the world of printing has been critical to my appreciation of the complete picture of our local book industry.

**Joel Cabrita:** Do you publish all your books in Nigeria, or do you send things to be published outside of the country?

**Lola Shoneyin:** Everything that we're not co-publishing with an international publishing house is printed and published in Nigeria. That's one of the things that I was particular about when I started Ouida Books. Again, it's about changing people's minds. Around 2015, it was the trend for many Nigerian publishers to print in India, China or somewhere else. I am of the view that we can only improve the quality of books produced by collectively setting high standards. My tweet today was 'I'm just really happy that more publishers are now printing in Nigeria.'

It didn't come easy, and the journey was rocky. We've had to pulp thousands of books because they weren't good enough to present to the public. Each time we had to do this, we'd return to the drawing board to figure out what went wrong. I spent a few years teaching the printer to care and pay attention to detail. A number of publishers are printing books in Nigeria

---

[2]    Shomolu is the printing capital of Lagos State, Nigeria.

now. The printer I work with even calls himself a publisher now.

**Joel Cabrita:** You've created a rival...

**Lola Shoneyin:** I think it is great! I love it when that happens. Everyone wins.

**Joel Cabrita:** Just thinking about one particular institution – Ouida Books, your publishing house. If there was a single guiding vision when you started it that you still see persisting today, what is it? What animates it? What's your big idea behind it?

**Lola Shoneyin:** Discovering talent. Nigerian or African talent. And being able to make it a product that can be sold to other markets. It doesn't sit well with me that the West still has the power to determine which African writers should be read, or which writers deserve attention. Of course, they control much of the industry but the only way to change that is by discovering, editing, publishing and promoting local authors and excellent writing. This is how to create your own market. This is how to disrupt the industry in a way that will favour Africans and give them the dignity they deserve. I take inspiration from our music industry. You can attend a party and have a fantastic time in Nigeria without playing a single track by a non-African musician. This was unheard of in my teenage years. I would love to see this happen in the Nigerian literary scene. It's about building a consumer base. Earning the trust of those consumers is key, so quality is critical. I would like us to publish works that will be enjoyed by African readers and acquired by other markets because they see their potential.

What normally happens is that Nigerian publishers have to grovel to acquire the rights to publish books that were authored by Nigerian writers. When we approach the larger publishing houses, we are bombarded with ridiculous reasons for denying African publishers such rights. Publishers in the West are quick to cite piracy as a reason for rejecting offers and bids from African publishers. Yes, there's piracy. There are certain types of nonfiction and biographies that are indeed produced illegally, but someone sent me the PDF of Hillary Clinton's book and James Comey's book via WhatsApp! Those PDFs did not originate from the African continent. The discrimination we endure from publishers is horrid. UK publishers who happily sell the rights of books to other English-speaking markets like America will suddenly get jittery when those same rights are sought for an English-speaking market in Africa.

**Joel Cabrita:** If they're not selling the rights, how are they imagining those books reach West African audiences?

**Lola Shoneyin:** When we have been able to get the rights, we have sold the books – some we've sold over 5,000 copies, the editions that we've produced in Nigeria. Otherwise, what the publishers do is to insist on a co-pub [co-publishing agreement]. Or they sell the books at  discounted prices but insist on a minimum of 1,000 copies. This means African booksellers are still buying their products. And I have seen instances where there is a stark difference in the paper quality of the books that Western publishers send to co-publishers.

The vision is to discover talent, to ensure that writers have publishing options in Nigeria, and to provide alternatives to depending solely on other markets. *An Abundance of*

*Scorpions* by Hadiza Isma El-Rufai was our first book that hadn't been published previously in the West. I worked with the author as her editor and published this book. We've sold over 5,000 copies in Nigeria alone. We've also recently sold the Arabic rights to Rewayat in the United Arab Emirates.[3] It's almost like creating a new literary Silk Road, because the current one has become oppressive. I was on a panel at the Sharjah International Book Fair in the UAE, and I mentioned that denying African publishers the opportunity to acquire the rights of books (authored by Africans) would eventually leave Western publishers with egg on their faces.

**Joel Cabrita:** I'd love to hear more about the money side of things. With almost all the publishers we've spoken with, a constant theme has been that it's really hard financially. It's hard to make sales and it's hard to navigate crumbling institutional structures like the mail service that handle distribution. There are a lot of challenges in the way of the publishing house becoming a lucrative business. I'd love to hear your thoughts on that.

**Lola Shoneyin:** Zukiswa Wanner negotiated a deal with DHL, making it possible to courier books around the continent at a slightly reduced rate. This is wonderful and it opens so many possibilities. But the truth is that we're constantly having to rebuild infrastructure that's not really our business to build. It's sad that we cannot rely on the Nigerian Postal Service – you send a book to a customer using the postal service but they

---

3   Rewayat is an imprint of UAE's Kalimat Group which publishes Arabic translations of Capote, McEwan, Baldwin, Al Bishr etc.

don't get the book. Zukiswa also created a WhatsApp group called 'BookFam Africa' with a long list of African publishers and booksellers. This means if you're in South Africa and you are interested in stocking a Ouida book from Nigeria, we are only a WhatsApp message away.

To be honest with you, I have sunk a lot of my personal resources into this work. There are times that I've run into debt because of it. It's one of the reasons why I have to take on other work. I work as a consultant for Sterling, a bank in Nigeria. Most of the extra funds I earn go into growing Ouida Books, taking care of my overheads. I'm extremely self-critical. I rarely sit and watch things happen around me. The way I control my environment is by helping to build the world I want to live in. I love this idea of people around me feeling and being empowered to believe that they can do things, especially young women. If I can model what is possible with my can-do, must-do attitude, then I have half succeeded. When people ask me, 'What's success for you?' I say it is being able to eat what I want, when I want. So if I feel like having sushi, I want to be able to afford it. If I am in the mood for roasted yam that costs less than a dollar, I want to be able to eat it and feel good about myself. I need money but my needs are quite basic. I am allergic to gold, and my love for comfort means certain material things often do not make it onto my need-to-have list.

**Joel Cabrita:** I'd like to end with a more personal question: I'm wondering if you have a religious faith, because a lot of the things you describe seem to be very moral visions about working for the collective good, about not pursuing personal self-interest, giving, generosity, and service. Where do these ideals come from for you?

**Lola Shoneyin:** I'm totally irreligious. I've been an atheist twenty-four years. I'm a rare African in the sense that I don't engage with organized religion, I don't go to church, I don't believe in a higher power or a supreme being. I think I was born without that gene. However, I do have faith in the capacity of human beings to be creative, to be resilient, to be ambitious, to be kind, and to do what is beneficial and considerate to the needs of the vulnerable. My ideals come from being human, and the understanding that if we don't fix our environment, we pay for it and our children do too. You can throw a sense of duty in there too. I feel incredibly lucky. I love my work. It doesn't feel like work. To be able to work in an area that brings together education, reading, literacy, culture, history – all the things that I love – is a daily gift. And I am very happy to share that gift.

**About Lola Shoneyin:** Lola is a publisher, bookseller and festival organizer, as well as a poet and writer. Her debut novel, *The Secret Lives of Baba Segi's Wives* (2010), was longlisted for the Women's Prize for Fiction and won the PEN/ Oakland Josephine Miles Literary Award and the ANA Ken Saro-Wiwa Prose Prize (all 2011). In 2013, Lola founded the Ake Arts and Book Festival in Nigeria. Ouida Books was founded in 2016. She is currently the director of Book Buzz Foundation, Nigeria – an NGO whose main aim is to promote literacy, develop reading spaces, and organize literary and cultural events..

*'I think that just the act of publishing
women is political.'*

---

# IN CONVERSATION WITH:
# COLLEEN HIGGS

19 August 2021

**Joel Cabrita:** Tell us about the founding of Modjaji Books in 2007. Why did you found it? How did you found it?

**Colleen Higgs:** I'd never worked in publishing before I started my own press. At that time, I was working at the Centre for the Book, an organization that was part of our national library, based in Cape Town.[1] My background is English as a second language education and high school teaching. I did a number of other things, but all related to education and training. I'm also a writer myself. And as a writer, I experienced the gatekeeping that happens. This was in a very small sector of publishing in South Africa, literary magazines. I was criticized as being too confessional, in terms of the poetry I wrote. I was working with Robert Berold who was the editor of *New Coin*, a local literary

---

[1] https://www.nlsa.ac.za/?page_id=23.

and poetry magazine. I helped him in an invisible way to edit
the magazine. At one point, he was asked to put together an
anthology of South African poetry. Robert included one of my
poems, but then one of the readers – these were all white men
who were making these decisions –told him to take out my
poem.

One weird example of pervasive gatekeeping was from a
Women's Day poetry reading. I was living in Grahamstown
(now called Makhanda) at the same period when I was working
with Robert. There was a little poetry reading, convened by a
professor who was a white man. All of us read some poems.
When I finished reading, he said, 'Thank you, Colleen. It's
so interesting how, unlike me, you don't use metaphor.' I
experienced these slights here and there that I think are now
called microaggressions. I've had a lot of that. That was one
of the reasons that I decided I wanted to start my own press.
I knew what it felt like and I imagined that it must be even
more so to the power of ten, even a hundred, for a Black South
African woman. I use the term 'Black' in the way that it used
to be used here, meaning everybody except for white people, a
political term.

At the Centre for the Book, I got to do this amazing project
called the Community Publishing Project (CPP) funded by one
of the big publishers. Hannes van Zyl, CEO at that time of NB
Publishers, had this dream. He came to the Centre for the Book
and said, 'Look, I've got some funding, and this is what I want
to do.' It was to give writers' groups or individual writers a very
small amount of money. We would then assist them in self-
publishing, because he thought this would be a way of building
a more diverse culture of reading and writing and publishing.

At that time in South Africa, the early 2000s, self-publishing wasn't as big as it is now. People submitted their manuscripts and we went through them and chose one, then gave them a small amount of money for a print run of 200 or 300 copies at the most. They had to try and source help then with the editing and book design. I loved the project and self-published my first collection of poems at the same time. Partly as a way of seeing if it was doable, what were the pros and cons, and also to be clearer about what I was trying to convey. I had many conversations with writers because of this part of my job. I found myself saying the same things over and over. I wrote all the advice up into a ten-page Word document. And then slowly, I developed it into a little book, and we got funding to have it translated into four other local languages. It was called *A Rough Guide to Small-scale and Self-publishing*.

In publishing my own first collection of poems, as well as the work with the CPP, I got bitten by the publishing bug. Then I had a child. In South Africa, and particularly with middle-class state schools, there's the expectation that either the mother or a caretaker can fetch kids at the drop of a hat. You're told that next week school is going to close at twelve instead of three, or we're going to have a swimming gala at this time. It's difficult to have the kind of job where you actually have to clock in and out. There was a bureaucratic element to my job at the Centre for the Book that didn't work for me. I wanted to leave that environment. It had become too oppressive for me, and I wanted the flexibility of working from home and had the mad idea that I could actually do this.

One of the things I would do differently now would be to set Modjaji up as a non-profit. Because of my work at the Centre for the Book, I'd done fundraising, document writing, and kind of hated it. So I thought it would be easier to have a business instead of a non-profit. But actually, there's a whole lot of administration and bureaucracy that comes with running a business. Maybe you don't have to write funding proposals, but you do still have to understand how financial management and accounts work. That's one of my weaknesses.

**Kyle Wang:** I wanted to circle back a little bit to the question of poetry. As a writer, you've published both prose and poetry. Have you found both as a writer and a publisher that publishing poetry contains a unique set of pressures that are different from publishing prose or fiction? And do you think it's more gatekept as a field?

**Colleen Higgs:** There's this kind of preciousness, I guess, about poetry publishing. Once again, it's partly gossip and sort of what one hears on the backchannel about some of the things I've published – the idea that things wouldn't be published if it hadn't been for Modjaji and not in a good way. I haven't accepted new poetry submissions for three years, because I've had a backlog of poetry books that I had committed to publishing. But it is also not really a financially viable thing to do. I don't think you could be a poetry press in South Africa and actually live off that work. The best you could hope for was that you cover your costs. New little presses rise up and then disappear all the time. Very few presses last beyond their founder, I think that's particularly true for poetry.

**Joel Cabrita:** For my part, I'd love to hear more about money. This is a theme that's cropped up time and again with many of the publishers we've spoken to – the financial challenges of starting a publishing company as well as the discussion about whether their company is for-profit or not-for-profit. Louise Umutoni spoke about wanting to be a commercial enterprise rather than a charity. She felt strongly that a press should be commercially viable, that there be some market demand for the product. Louise also referenced the anxiety about donors calling the tune in terms of topics or subject matter and sacrificing or compromising publishing autonomy. Obviously you've chosen the business route for Modjaji, but I imagine there are still tensions in running it as a business rather than a non-profit.

**Colleen Higgs:** I agree with Louise. I think it's important to have a business focus as a publisher. I'll give you some examples of what can happen when you don't. Some years ago, our Department of Arts and Culture founded a literary magazine called *Baobab*. They must have thrown money at this project. But it didn't last. There were maybe eight issues or even fewer. They used this expensive thick paper, and the production values were through the roof. It was full colour, beautiful photographs, and artwork. But the magazine cost next to nothing to buy, maybe thirty rands or twenty-five rands. It was just crazy, I think a much better way to spend money would be to buy subscriptions for literary magazines that already exist for all libraries, even for school libraries.

Countries like the Netherlands and Canada fund publishing by buying books from publishers for public libraries. We do have public libraries buying our books, but I'll be lucky if a hundred copies will be bought nationally for libraries. And we have about 1,500 public libraries. Obviously there has to be some selection, because there are a lot of second-rate books that get published and every book in South Africa can't be bought by the scheme. But even if 500 copies of selected titles were bought, that would just change everything. I would be able to employ a full-time editorial person and assistant and rent space. I'd have bigger print runs, books would be cheaper, it would just change everything. But I don't know if that's ever going to happen. One book I've published will have been out for a year in October and I think we've sold 700 copies. So it's not great. But it's not bad for a debut author. I have had other books that have sold much better. A lot of the books that I've published have had a long tail, so to speak. Later on, they might get prescribed. And we continue with social media publicity so older titles stay alive.

Yeah, money has been a nightmare for me. I have basically shot myself in the foot in terms of my retirement. I'm turning sixty in January and I have no pension to speak of. I imagined that when I started Modjaji, that it was going to work out and that somehow it wouldn't be as financially insecure as it is. Modjaji looks good, the website, the titles, the prizes, the kinds of authors I've published, who've gone on to do other more fantastic things. Covid has just had a terrible impact on the South African economy. Turnover has dropped to about a third of what it was pre-lockdown. Even then things weren't rosy. So I've been taking on a lot of assisted self-publishing projects and using that to fund Modjaji. I've had no fixed salary since Modjaji started, no salary where I know exactly, 'This is how much I'm going to get each month'. No, it's like, 'I can only be paid after I've paid many other invoices first'. It hasn't been financially easy at all. I'm not really a business person. I mean, I've had to learn to be one. But there's still a lot more that I could learn about that.

**Joel Cabrita:** I'm sorry it's been such a tough time. The economic impact of Covid must be devastating. It's illuminating to hear you speak so frankly about the financial challenges because this is the reality facing each and every small independent publisher on the continent. What are the specifics of the South African reading market? Why are sales lower than you'd like? Is it because of people's budgets? And is it that particularly right now, during Covid, people just don't have disposable income to spend on a book?

**Colleen Higgs:** I think it's all of those things. I saw an article today that mentioned how the South African middle class is really battling. They would be the buyers of books. And that class is battling in this pandemic. So that's not good news for a publisher, unless the state commits to buying a certain number of books for public libraries.

Also, there have been a lot of interesting and exciting changes happening in South Africa. There have been some huge successes with self-publishing. There's a writer Dudu Busani Dube, who has a background in journalism and marketing, and that's her work. And she's written a series of popular books. She sells tens of thousands of copies of her books. And they're the same price as my books. It's two different markets. The South African bookshop market has got a traditional customer base, which has expanded and grown in the last twenty years. But she's reached other readers and has used different tactics for reaching them. I don't know exactly what she has done, but certainly she seems to be well-placed. Exclusive Books, our biggest upmarket chain of bookshops, who've also been battling during Covid, initially didn't want to stock her book. But there was such demand from readers clamouring to get hold of her book. And it's been a best seller in bookshops. At first Dudu did all her own distribution, but it became a full-time job so she moved to a distributor who markets and distributes to bookshops and collects the money.

Also, here in South Africa there has been a practice of sale or return. Exclusive Books have been doing huge returns during this [Covid] period. It's a nightmare, because you think you've sold a book and you've had this much money in, but then it turns out that you didn't and you haven't. So that's been hard.

Also, one of the oldest stationers and bookstores [CNA] has been put under financial receivership. I'm sure that I'm a candidate for being under financial receivership. I just somehow managed to keep afloat. I think it's because we're such a small organization and it's really just me. Somehow one can just keep going. Whereas when you've got a lot of staff in stores, and rent to malls and so on, you come under much more scrutiny. I've also been lucky in the sense that I've had a lot of support and interest and enthusiasm for what I've been doing. The service providers who work with me are often lenient in terms of not necessarily being paid within thirty days. They give me a bit more leeway. But during Covid most of the printers that I work with changed their terms to insisting that I've got to pay before the books leave the warehouse. That's been tough. In publishing, there's a lot of investment upfront and it takes quite a while to get any of the money back from that investment. You know, your sales into bookshops, it takes ninety days from the time the books land in the warehouse, and they become back orders. Those back orders are never huge.

**Kyle Wang:** You've described extensively how it's not easy to survive in any kind of literary publishing worlds. Is there a sense of community or solidarity between publishers themselves? Or do you think it's always been a kind of contested landscape?

**Colleen Higgs:** Obviously, there are little jealousies and rivalries. But also the other way around. On the whole my experience with other publishers is that there's a kind of collegiality, sharing of information, and encouraging each other. The most supportive community of publishers are those I've met through the Frankfurt Book Fair's Invitation Programme. I've got publishing friends in places like Brazil and Uganda and different Latin American countries. It's only other third-world countries, so to speak, that get to be part of that programme. Also, since 2014, Modjaji has been a member of the International Alliance of Independent Publishers. So I've made new colleagues and friends, and it's wonderful to be supported there. In some ways, I feel that my experience is that the work that Modjaji has done is more enthusiastically received as a concept and body of work overseas than it is here. Not necessarily by other publishers but by the wider community of people who are interested in this work. It may also just be the fact that I am oddly enough more connected to those interested international colleagues than to local ones. The work is quite isolating, you know, because I work here in my home. One is connected through emails and WhatsApp and social media, but in terms of actually physically having people around, who are doing the same thing... no.

**Joel Cabrita:** Let's shift our discussion more to the broader political context that you're working within. Could you think with us about how you situate Modjaji Books in a longer history of South African publishing, particularly publishing that had an explicitly political or revolutionary agenda to it? That's such a strong theme in South African publishing history.

**Colleen Higgs:** I feel like Modjaji is a slightly mad and audacious thing that I've done, because it's really just been me who decided to do it. But I do still see it as being part of the longer history – the kind of publishing that presses like Ravan did was very important. But when Modjaji started in 2007, it was a different time, and I wanted to publish women in particular. The personal is the political. So, in a sense, unlike some other feminist presses, like Spinifex in Australia, whom I admire hugely, Modjaji is about publishing voices of the ordinary woman. Some of them become extraordinary, or maybe they always were, but are more visible from the opportunity of having been published. I was interested in ordinary people's experiences and stories they've come up with, within the traditional genres of novels and short stories and memoirs. Obviously the politics of the time emerge through that. I think that just the act of publishing women is political. There has been a little bit of a fight-back, but not actually as much as I would have expected. Some people who like what the press does don't even realize that we literally only publish women.

But things have changed a lot since I first started publishing. Now some of the bigger or mainstream publishing companies (Modjaji is a micro press really, in terms of budget and capacity), have started to publish the kinds of things that interested me. Jonathan Ball has just brought out an anthology about gender-based violence, different women's stories as narrative nonfiction. To me, it is noteworthy that they decided to publish a title like that. There's been a big shift. Modjaji has been part of that. And obviously, it's part of a much bigger awareness that's been happening in the world, especially in the last few years with the hashtags (#metoo) and the sort of things that are challenged now, and where people like Woody Allen were called into question. We're very influenced in South Africa with what goes on in the UK and the United States. People often know more about the US, than about what's going on here, because it's more in the media. I'm talking about a certain sector of the population as well, the population on social media.

**Joel Cabrita:** Across the continent, are there any other African presses that publish only women?

**Colleen Higgs:** I could be wrong, but I don't think so. Also, in the last few years, the issue of trans women has come up. I say to people that you can submit to us if you are a woman or identify as a woman. But I haven't had any manuscripts from trans women. And there have been a couple published in South Africa, Jonathan Ball published one, a memoir.

**Joel Cabrita:** I noticed on your website that your eligibility requirement is that you'd be a Southern African woman for your manuscript to be considered by Modjaji. Can you speak to the kind of politics around feminism at this moment? We are in a moment where gender binaries are being increasingly questioned and broken down. I'm curious to know what that means for a press that has invested its identity in the idea of womanhood. How do you see feminism responding to these new conversations about gender that are happening?

**Colleen Higgs:** I still feel that in South Africa, there is room for what Modjaji is doing. It's a very patriarchal, very conservative society. Our statistics in terms of rape and gender-based violence are catastrophic. It's still so important that women are empowered and their voices, our voices, are given space and amplified. That's one part of the work – a tiny part, but important, I think – of changing our society. Thank goodness we don't have [Jacob] Zuma as our president now. He was accused of rape shortly before he came into office. So just having Zuma as president of our country didn't do anything for women's rights and it was like stepping back many decades. Thankfully, now we've got a different president and there's a different sense of the world. I don't think the statistics have improved, but there's a feeling that we can do something here. It's not just hopeless. Currently Modjaji's focus is to make space for voices that don't get enough airtime and to redress the way in which women, particularly Black women, have been silenced.

**Kyle Wang:** Thank you for that answer. When you were talking about women's issues during the Zuma presidency, it made me wonder whether you see publishers in general as possessing a kind of social responsibility?

**Colleen Higgs** I do, I do. But I don't know that all publishers see it quite like that. The books that sell the best in South Africa are biographies of sports people, historical figures, or biographies, memoirs that have a tabloid-ish feel to them. This is trade publishing. Within English publishing in South Africa, and in terms of our readers, we are competing with international publishing. Because those publishers can do big print runs, often their books are cheaper, even though they are imported.

I got side-tracked, but back to your question about social

responsibility. To some extent, that has been the case in South Africa, with Ravan Press, David Philip, those kinds of publishers, Lovedale Press. Publishers in South Africa, but maybe elsewhere as well, are largely politically progressive. Obviously, it's not 100 per cent true, but also there are other things that have come into play in South Africa. Identity politics is big here. To me it promotes a conservative agenda, even though the people who might be expressing it or living it wouldn't necessarily think they were conservative. I'm a kind of old lefty. From the 80s. That was when I came to political awareness.

**Joel Cabrita:** Along those lines, there's gender but there are also of course ongoing debates around identity politics and race. One of the questions that we've asked publishers we've spoken to is how they define 'African', because many have had a remit to publish the work of African authors. So we've been interested in how publishers have variously defined African, whether they count Africans living in the diaspora or second or third generation Africans or whether you have to be resident somewhere on the continent. We'd be interested to hear more from you about how you define Southern African and obviously, Southern Africa is unique in the context of the continent having a declining but still quite large white population. I think you alluded earlier to that inclusive sense of Blackness. Steve Biko wrote about Blackness as a political statement and that it's a form of solidarity, rather than a kind of biological determinant. I'm not really asking you a specific question as much as requesting to hear more about how you're thinking about race as a white woman in publishing at this particular moment in South Africa.

**Colleen Higgs:** There isn't just one thing to say, or one answer. I think it's complicated. So I see myself as Southern African or South African. But I also understand why that might be seen as problematic for some interest groups. We had that violent phrase, before the end of apartheid: 'One settler, one bullet'. Generations back, my family were settlers. But it's hard to feel like a settler now when, on both sides of my family we have lived here for many generations. In a similar vein, one could argue that most Americans are not really Americans. Like only Native Americans are American. I think there are unhelpful ways to think about things. But I understand that in South Africa, particularly, we have this history of apartheid. I'm not going to be one to go on to social media and have debates about South African identity and being white. I just don't think what I have to say about these issues is that important. I think that there's a lot of room to just work and to do things that say something without having to explicitly go around having arguments. It's an easy place to be as a white person in South Africa, even to do the work that I'm doing. And I'm sure that there are people who think I shouldn't be doing what I've done, or certainly shouldn't do it now that there are other publishers who are doing similar work. Sometimes social media voices can be frightening, but actually, is that what everyone thinks? I did see when I first started that an important thing to do was to publish Black women writers. But that has shifted enormously since I've started publishing. So it doesn't feel quite as urgent as it did then. So I can publish other things. It doesn't have to be the first determinant, so to speak.

**Joel Cabrita:** Do you exclusively publish Black women?

**Colleen Higgs:** No, I've probably published more white women, not because I've wanted to, but the conditions are such that in general white women have more time and space to write, even though they're a smaller percentage of the population. Maybe there's wealth in the home or they can be supported, and they've got time. In fact, I've often turned down really good manuscripts because I feel like, okay, I've got enough [white authors]. There's the pool of people that I work with, this group of readers helps me to select the writers to publish. You can't publish everything that there is to publish, even if it's good enough. So you have to choose. Also, the manuscript that you get versus the manuscript that you publish, it's been through a lot of work to get to that point. So at that manuscript stage, it's not always completely clear which one is the most amazing. Obviously, there's a voice. But quite a few of the books that I've published have had a lot of work that's happened after selection.

**Joel Cabrita:** That's a suggestive place to end this discussion – the idea that however radical they are, in the end, publishers themselves also replicate these gatekeeping dynamics. It seems unavoidable because, as you say, there's a work of selection and sifting and rejection that inevitably goes on. It's unclear whether any publisher – however progressive or ambitious – can ever stay aloof from these uncomfortable political or power dynamics.

**About Colleen Higgs:** Colleen is a writer and publisher. Her writing includes poetry, short stories and memoir. She has had four books published and her work has been anthologized and has appeared in literary magazines in South Africa since the 1990s. Her most recent book is a memoir, *my mother, my madness* (2020). After a long career as an educator and a role in managing the Centre for the Book in Cape Town, Colleen founded Modjaji Books in 2007 as 'an independent feminist press that publishes Southern African women writers'. Currently, Modjaji Books publishes short stories, novels, poetry, creative nonfiction and memoirs.

*'What does it take to be a writer?
To be a woman writer? To be an African
woman writer? What will it take for
us to tell our stories?'*

## IN CONVERSATION WITH: GORETTI KYOMUHENDO

8 September 2021

**Joel Cabrita:** You're a fiction writer but you also occupy the mantle of a literary activist working to enrich reading and literacy culture. How have your dual identities as a fiction writer and as literary activist developed in tandem with each other, or was it fiction writer first or literary activist second?

**Goretti Kyomuhendo:** Writing is my first love, so before the activism was the writing. For me, activism is something that I needed to do, whereas writing is my passion. Writing is my love. But activism is something that I have to do. There was a point where my activism overtook my writing, and that used to bother me. But I think now I've found a balance between the two. I published my first novel twenty-five years ago as of this year [2021]. It was published in 1996, and my activism started soon after that, because when you operate and work in a marginalized context or culture, I think it is inevitable for you to involve [yourself] in acts of activism. I used to look at my marginalized context from two angles. First was being an African woman and second was being a writer and publisher on the African continent.

So why is this? Because one, the publishing industry on the continent is still underdeveloped. It does not have sufficient structures to support the growth and development of a writer, because of narrow and small markets, because of lack of facilities, because of the difficulties and limitations of the movement of books and writers between different countries. As a writer, I found myself starting to do the work a publisher should [really] do. I started promoting my own work, and alongside that, promoting other writers' works. Second, I was working as a woman, as an African woman writer. When we started FEMRITE in 1996, this coincided with the publication of my first novel [*The First Daughter*]. [At the time] there were hardly any Ugandan women writers who had been published because of various issues. So we had to start from nothing. We had to start by doing everything: the promotion, the development, the training to get skills, publishing our own work, promoting it, selling it, everything. We were the first group on the literary scene in Uganda. To go back to your question, for me the two go hand in hand – I wear both hats. I acknowledge and accept both identities because I've not separated one from the other.

**Joel Cabrita:** Can you speak in more detail about some of the challenges women writers in very male-dominated literary scenes face? What challenges specifically as a woman writer have you faced and continue to face?

**Goretti Kyomuhendo:** For me, one of the difficulties that we faced as Ugandan women writers was [the] lack of personal empowerment to tell our stories. Because there was no shortage of stories – almost all the women writers had the basic skill and talent to tell the stories – but there was a lack of confidence, of empowerment, to tell those stories. I'll give you an example. Usually, in an African context, a woman's identity is constructed [by] using that of another. A woman would be referred to or identified as the 'mother of' somebody and take on that identity and that name. If you have a son called John, for example, you would be identified as 'Mama John'. And if you are a married woman in some African cultures, actually, you take on a prefix of your husband's name. The prefix 'muka' means 'wife of'. That's different from being 'Mrs so-and-so'. If your husband is Brian, your name might change to 'Muka-Brian', the 'Wife of Brian'. So all these multiple identities create a sense of responsibility, a sense of weight on your shoulders as a woman.

When you start writing, these are the issues that come to you. And you must scrutinize everything you are writing. How can you write a story with explicit sexual connotations, for example, if you are mother of John, and probably John is now a teenager, and you are the wife of so-and-so, and also the daughter of your father. These things used to prohibit women from telling the stories in their hearts, because of a lack of confidence to tell the actual stories that they would want to tell. We had a woman at FEMRITE who had written a very beautiful story. I still remember the opening line even twenty-five years later. It read, 'I was raped on my wedding night.' And I remember sitting up and saying, 'What a beautiful opening line.' The story went on in the first-person narrative voice. But she said that when she showed it to her husband, the husband said to her, 'But people are going to think it's you my wife who was raped on our wedding night! And that raises the question – by whom? By me? By my brother? By my father? By my relatives?' And she had to change that story and write it in the third person: 'Angela was raped on her wedding night.' Of course, that lost all the impact and the beauty of that first line. Some of the activities we did at FEMRITE were to empower the women to tell their stories. Some of the workshops we started with were personal empowerment workshops: what does it mean to be a writer? What does it take to be a writer? To be a woman writer? To be an African woman writer? What will it take for us to tell those stories?

**Joel Cabrita:** That moves us seamlessly into the work that you did in founding and directing FEMRITE in the late 1990s. From what you've said, we already have a sense of the reason behind the founding of FEMRITE. Could we now hear more about the logistics of it? Who were the other women that you were working with and how did you find each other and come up with this idea for an organization supporting women writers from Uganda and East Africa as a whole?

**Goretti Kyomuhendo:** The whole idea was mooted by a lady called Mary Korooro-Okurut. She was a lecturer at Makerere University teaching literature. Because she was working with these young female students who were writing, she also saw the potential of bringing together other women writers. First of all, for the group she was teaching at the university but also looking around for other women writers that might want to join the association. As I have mentioned, at that time I had just published my first novel, and [Mary] had heard of it, because it was being reviewed and talked about, and being taught in some of the schools. She got to know about me through my book (in fact, Mary was one of those who reviewed it), and contacted me and told me about this idea. Of course, I wholly supported it, because I myself had struggled to write and publish my novel. At that time – the mid-1990s – there was only one mainstream publishing house in Uganda, Fountain Publishers. And it had been a big struggle for me to publish with them. It took years for the novel to get published. Even when it had been accepted, [Fountain Publishers] had to raise the funds to publish the novel. I had to get involved in looking for the money. So I really welcomed this idea that as women we could come together and support each other. In 1997, I became the director of FEMRITE. We were just women writers joining together to form and run this association. We didn't have any skills of fundraising, of writing funding proposals and budgets, of doing the logistical frameworks – [of] all that business. We had no idea. We were just driven by passion for publishing and love for the work we were doing.

For probably the first three years, we operated on a zero budget. We used to meet under a tree in Kampala because we had no office. We had nothing. But the group kept growing by word of mouth and just through us talking to people. Then the media got interested in what we were doing, so they did a lot of publicity for us. After around two or three years, we were discovered by Hivos, a Dutch funding agency. They had heard about us, and they were in Uganda looking for arts and literary organizations [to fund]. At that time, we were just about the only group in the country that was promoting literature. So funding came to us.

The women who were involved with FEMRITE were in three categories. There was the young group from the university who were mainly writing short stories or poetry. But there were also a couple of women who already had manuscripts. The third category were those few women who had managed to publish their books before coming to FEMRITE. But these were just a handful, really, three or four women at most. There were more women who had written and not published. Some of them had about three manuscripts which they had written and finished and put away. And when we asked them why they didn't look for publishers – okay, there was only one mainstream publishing house in the country, but I had managed to publish my novel – they would just say, 'I didn't think it was good enough. We didn't think anybody would be interested.' This was very revealing for us. Immediately, we realized we could not just talk about writing, not just train these women in personal empowerment and writing skills – we had to publish these books, the manuscripts that they [already] had. Two or three years later, we launched a publishing house – FEMRITE Publications Limited – and we started publishing. That would have been in 1998 or 1999. There was a year we published five novels. So we just kept going because the women were writing. Right now, there are over thirty titles, with at least one title published every year. These are mainly anthologies, collections of creative nonfiction, and thematic stories written by FEMRITE members on topical issues like HIV/AIDS, migration and refugees, and so on.

Most of the things we did were learnt on the job, such as understanding what editing meant, and printing, and selling. I remember our first challenge was after we had printed probably 2,000 copies or more of three titles. So we had about 6,000 copies. But we had no storage. So that was something we hadn't imagined. We didn't know about [the importance of planning for storage]. I remember the printer calling me and saying, 'We have finished printing your books.' I said, 'But we have nowhere to store all of them.' We hadn't thought about that or budgeted for it. So I said, 'There's only one way, which is to try and sell these books.' Everybody ended up getting involved. So the FEMRITE group – at that time we would've been about forty women – each one was tasked with trying to sell off these books, because we had no storage. Those were some of the things we were learning on the job.

**Joel Cabrita:** What do you attribute the lack of a local publishing scene in Uganda to? I know one of your neighbours, Tanzania, had a fairly vibrant publishing industry in the 1980s and 1990s (I'm thinking of people like Walter Bgoya and others). So why not in Uganda?

**Goretti Kyomuhendo:** It stems back to the early '60s when Uganda gained her independence from the British. Uganda got independence in 1962, and around that time, we were the literary hub of the continent. Everything literary happened in Uganda. The first African Writers' Conference was hosted in Uganda at Makerere University in 1962. This was the very first ever African Writers' Conference of those writers working in English, and it was attended by all the literary heavyweights. Chinua Achebe was there, Ngũgĩ wa Thiong'o, Ama Ata Aidoo, Christopher Okigbo, Wole Soyinka – all the big writers, or those who would become important in the future, were at that conference. Soon after that, the ACLALSC [Association of Commonwealth Literature and Languages Studies Conference] was also hosted at Makerere in the early '70s. That was the first time that the conference was being hosted on the African continent. Then there was *Transition* magazine, which published all the big and important writers not only on the continent, but also beyond. It had also been established at Makerere in 1961. *Song of Lawino* by Okot P'Bitek was published in 1966, launching Ugandan literature (written in English) on the world scene. So things were happening. And Uganda – and Makerere as a university and Kampala as a city – was hosting all the important African writers. If you trace back, almost all of them have had a stay, or had a connection to Uganda in their literary lives. Professor Ali Mazuri was at Makerere, Ngũgĩ did his undergraduate studies at Makerere University, writers like Nuruddin Farah spent time in Uganda. So Uganda was the focal point for literary production. It attracted all the literary heavyweights in one way or the other. This was the '60s right through to the '70s. [But] all these names I am mentioning – they were all men. Women's voices were missing; they were not participating in this literary movement of the early '60s and early '70s.

But came Idi Amin, and everything collapsed. Three things happened to Ugandan writers during that time. Some of the writers were killed because of their work. The majority went into exile, most of them to neighbouring Kenya and Tanzania, but others fled to Europe, the US and Canada. The ones who remained in the country went silent, because it was too dangerous to write. So we had that [literary] vacuum which ran through the late '70s – because Idi Amin was overthrown in 1979 – through the '80s, up to the early '90s. Prior to Idi Amin, we had several multinational publishing houses in Uganda, including Oxford University Press, Macmillan, Longman, and others, but they had all fled during Idi Amin's reign. So we had this long dry period of nearly twenty years. So in the late '80s to the early '90s, when things started to pick up again, that's when Fountain Publishers was established, in 1988. Then some of the multinational publishing houses returned, some of them did not. And FEMRITE also came riding in on the back of this rejuvenation of [literary life] around 1995-1996.

**Joel Cabrita:** How did the work you did with FEMRITE then segue into your work with the African Writers Trust (which I think you founded in 2009)?

**Goretti Kyomuhendo:** I spent ten years at FEMRITE. For those ten years, I never had a [day of] leave, I never had a break. FEMRITE wasn't a job – it was my life. It was everything. We worked every day without rest. After ten years, I burnt out. I couldn't do it any more. Also, for personal reasons, I was moving to London around then. I remember telling myself, 'That's it, no more activism.' I was working on my next novel. I said to myself, 'I'm just going to write, and get an eight to five job.' And I did that. I survived for exactly one year in that job. It was around then that I founded the African Writers Trust. I think it was still the activism in me.

When I moved to London, I had begun to meet many African writers living in the diaspora. I remember my first job was working at the Southbank Centre. I was part of the team organizing the London Literature Festival and [in connection with this job], I would meet very many African writers [living in the UK]. During my work with FEMRITE, we used to travel extensively on the continent, attending book fairs, promoting our works, and so on. So I had got to know almost all of the African writers on the continent. Now talking to these writers in the diaspora, it hit me that there was a big disconnect between the two groups, between the writers who lived and worked on the continent, and the writers who left Africa, or were born in the diaspora. And [this latter group] almost never had the opportunity to return to the continent. There are many literary festivals and events that happen in the US and Europe, with a particular focus on African literature. For example, the African Literature Association conference in the US, the African Book Festival in Berlin, Africa Writes in London, and others. But there wasn't much to return these diaspora writers to the continent. And these African writers were well-established [in the diaspora]. They had benefited from a good education system. They had access to things like writers' grants, writers' fellowships, writers' residencies, even just books and information – all of which we lacked on the continent.

These diaspora writers were all eager to share their experiences, their knowledge, and the resources that they had with writers on the continent. That got me thinking: suppose I work towards bridging that divide [between continental and diaspora writers]? To me, it seemed more geographical than anything else. These writers still wrote stories from the continent, even those who had left as children. They still drew from the same epistemological space that the writers on the continent were inhabiting. They still talked about Africa. They still wanted to come back to Africa. In my conversations with them, they were mostly very eager. They said to me, 'If there was an opportunity, I would be happy to go to Africa and run a writers' workshop.' So that's how the African Writers Trust was founded. Essentially it exists to bridge these spaces that divide us.

Over the last ten years, I've invited several writers to deliver keynotes at the biennial International Writers' Conference that we host in Uganda. These include Jackie Kay, Lemn

Sissay, Jennifer Nansubuga Makumbi, Zakes Mda. Others like Margaret Busby, Ellah Wakatama, and Bibi Bakare-Yusuf have come to run editing and publishing workshops. I've worked with Colleen [Higgs] in South Africa. She hosted two interns at Modjaji Books in Cape Town who had completed our editorial skills development training programme. We don't only bring African writers. We also bring their books. We have a small online bookshop called Books First Uganda which stocks their books. We sell the books at affordable prices to Uganda and the rest of the region.

**Joel Cabrita:** One of the themes we've discussed with the visitors over the last year is the question of defining an 'African' writer. Is it someone who lives on the continent, or can it also include someone who has historic or family ties but lives in the diaspora? Your work with the African Writers Trust seems to be tackling those issues of identity full on. How do you grapple with these complexities around who an 'African' writer is?

**Goretti Kyomuhendo:** At the heart of what we do is dialogue – dialogue across the continent and dialogue across the diaspora. We do training and skills development workshops in writing, editing and publishing. But every two years we also hold an international writers' conference, as I've already mentioned, where we have between twenty-five and thirty writers both from the continent and the diaspora. So far, we've had four editions (the fifth edition would have been this year, if not for Covid). These conferences are about dialogue. For the writers who have remained on the continent, there is a level of misgivings towards the writers who left, whom they term as 'no longer part of us'. There's a Ugandan writer at the moment who is our most established and prominent, Jennifer Makumbi. [Makumbi] lives in Manchester, and she was our keynote speaker for our last conference. We were also launching her latest book. I remember the Ugandans asking her, 'Ah, you've lived away from Uganda since 2002, and in your book, you're writing about boda bodas (small motorcycles that transport people). What experience do you have of them? When you left they were not here, and now you're writing about them in your book. Who gives you the licence to write about these stories? You left, you're not part of the continent.' Also, diaspora writers are looked at [abroad] as ambassadors for the continent; living in Europe and the US, they represent the continent. They are also easier to invite to attend festivals in Europe or the US than a writer from the continent is, because of all the travel and visa restrictions. So for me, creating this dialogue and this platform is very important.

The writers in the diaspora also explain [to continent-based writers] the hardships that they go through. If you are an African writer living in the UK, it's very difficult to get published. They'll tell them, 'Do you know what it means to live outside my home, to miss my family?' We have created dialogue, which is very important. We don't want that division of 'these are African writers in the diaspora' versus 'African writers on the continent'. We can learn from one another, we can share experiences.

**Brittany Linus:** I find what you say very timely. I'm Nigerian, but I wasn't born on the continent. I had to struggle with that growing up, trying to figure out whether I am African-American or African. Out in the world, I present as African-American, but my cultural upbringing is that of a typical African. So recognition of that experience is something you bring to the table, I highly admire that, and I'm very grateful. My question is whether there is a particular genre you would love to see more writers publishing in? I'm particularly interested in fantasy and Afrofuturism.

**Goretti Kyomuhendo:** One of the genres I would be very keen to see more of is memoir writing, personal stories, life stories. I really think that is what is missing. As for speculative fiction, science fiction, afterlife – I think that is picking up. Many of the young writers we work with are operating in that genre. But I still feel that we are not telling our stories, our real personal stories. I know writers shouldn't be prescribed what to write, they should choose what to write, but I feel we are missing something. There is so much that has happened on the continent, and if we are not ready or happy to tell those stories, then somebody else is going to tell those stories for us. From Nigeria, there are the terrible kidnapping stories of schoolchildren. There are other ugly images of the continent. In Uganda we have our own share of that. We have had mass killings, wars, everything ugly. But I still feel that these stories deserve to be known, deserve to be listened to. And they don't only have to be the bad stories. People also have success stories, the young writers especially. And that is a genre that is completely missing: nonfiction, memoir, autobiography or biography. The most popular genres are poetry, and probably short fiction. We see a lot of that, but my reservation about that is most of the writers' skills are not yet up to a standard where these stories are told well enough for them to be competitive at an international standard. If people are helped to write their real-life stories, I feel we would do much better than we are doing in fiction.

**Barry Migott:** Goretti, you mentioned the 1960s being dominated by mostly male writers. But I grew up in Kenya and there were some female writers that I read at school, like Barbara Kimenye and Marjorie Oludhe Macgoye. What surprised me was that they were not African. What factors would have caused these women to come from Europe – Barbara to Uganda and Marjorie to Kenya? They became successful, yet not the African women writers.

**Goretti Kyomuhendo:** That's a difficult question. Before I answer, I'd like to mention another example of a successful Kenyan female writer, who actually was from the country – Grace Ogot, one of my favourite writers. I think it all goes back to what I was saying a moment ago, that we are still not writing our own stories. I think two issues prevent us from doing so. One, it's dangerous for an African writer to write about the politics of [their] country, unless you leave the country and go into exile. But second, probably these stories are still too close to us for comfort. They are too painful. We may also think they are not important, because they are our everyday experience. If you have been raised and grown up in a grass-thatched house, what is unique about it? Why should I write about it? It is someone coming from outside who has never seen a grass-thatched house who is going to write about that and put it in their stories.

**Kyle Wang:** You said earlier that you've always been a writer at heart, regardless of the literary activism that you do, and that writing is your core passion. How does your work as a writer shape your approach to the literary activism that you do? In retrospect, how has doing work in the literary activism space changed your relationship to the writing process?

**Goretti Kyomuhendo:** As I said, at a certain point my activism overtook my writing. I last published a novel in 2007. It was published by the Feminist Press in New York. Since then, I've been struggling to finish and publish my next novel. I've done a few short stories in between and children's books. But I haven't published a major novel. Looking back, I think it's because in 2009 I was working to establish the African Writers Trust. For the last ten years, it has been really hard work, trying to establish something from scratch. When I started African Writers Trust, there was nothing, just an idea. As we speak now, we have a fully fledged office in Kampala. I have five staff members. We do workshops every year. We do about five programmes – we do a conference, we do internships, we do mentoring, I bring in guests from America, from Norway, from everywhere. Now I'm beginning to get [more] balance. African Writers Trust is now at a level where I can step back and go back to my writing.

[But] it's difficult to separate the two [writing and activism]. As I said, if you work in a marginalized context, you take on much more than you should as a writer. When I write and publish a novel, I still have to make sure I find avenues of selling it. If I'm organizing a book launch, it's me organizing the book launch. If my last novel was published in the US, I still have to ensure that copies are available in Uganda. I have to write to the publisher, and then find ways of shipping it to Uganda. It really never stops. If we had a developed publishing industry with all the structures that support the growth of a writer, I wouldn't have to be doing all this. But when all that is missing, you find yourself getting involved in every little aspect of your work.

**Joel Cabrita:** It seems as if there's been a turnaround from the male-dominated period of the 1960s and 1970s – where all the literary luminaries you named were men – versus the situation today, where there are a great number of prominent African women writers. You said the most famous Ugandan novelist today is probably Jennifer Mukumbi. And this is the case not only in the writers' sphere, but also in the publishing world; for example, all the individuals we've interviewed for this project are women. What's going on here?

**Goretti Kyomuhendo:** I would start by saying that women are natural nurturers. If you look at the work of these women, a lot of it has to do with nurturing, mentoring, handholding. As women, we are very good at that. It comes to us naturally. Also, women make things happen. I really believe that. There were hardly any women writers at the Makerere conference of 1962. I think Ama Ata Aidoo, the Ghanaian writer, was there. I think Efua Sutherland was also there as well as Micere Mugo from Kenya.[1] But that was about it. [Yet] that doesn't mean that there were no women writers or that there were no women literary activists. I think [rather] that they were suppressed by the dominance of the male writers. But it doesn't mean they were not in existence. So when the platforms arrived to support them and to promote them, [women writers] just sprung up.

---

[1]   Grace Ogot and Rebecca Njau from Kenya and Ghana's Elizabeth Spio-Garbra were the women writers who attended the Conference of African Writers of English Expression at Makerere in 1962. The other woman was Frances Ademola, a Ghanaian broadcaster who was based in Nigeria at the time.

Also, women in the African context are the traditional storytellers: it's not the men, it's the women. I got my own storytelling passion and skills from my grandmother. My grandmother used to sit us around the fire because that was our only form of entertainment – there was no television, no movies, there was nothing – and so she told stories. And that's where I picked up my passion and love for storytelling. But what happened to her stories? Her stories were folktales, they were imaginary, they were fairy tales, they were transient. So they were not regarded as important as my grandfather's. Because my grandfather used to tell stories too, but not in the home setting, not around the fire. My grandfather would tell stories in the public domain, in a bar, in the village bar, at a wrestling ground, and these were heroic stories. For example, he'd narrate stories of coming back from winning a war, a conflict between tribes – those are the stories he and other men used to tell. These were regarded as the important stories. They would talk about hunting, having killed a lion, coming back home with the lion's head. My grandmother's tales were regarded as frivolous: 'Oh, those are women's stories; oh, those are fairy tales; those are imaginary; those are things that don't exist. Those are not important stories.'

Looking from that era to the present day, women's stories are still not regarded as that important. Women write about love, women are romantics. You've heard of women writers who've had to take on a man's name to write and get published. Our voices are still missing because of that lack of promotion, that lack of support, lack of empowerment, that lack of confidence. Just like my grandmother was not accorded that platform. [Her stories were told] round the fire and the fireplace and the small kitchen, and we the grandchildren listening to her. Nobody else knew she was a wonderful storyteller. Yet people would talk about [male storytellers] because they would publicly recite [their stories].

**Joel Cabrita:** The devaluing that you describe – whereby certain genres associated with women writers are demeaned – reminds me of a conversation we had with Zukiswa Wanner. She was talking about how the label of 'chick lit' often gets attached to her work, somehow implying it's a 'lesser' literary genre. She made the point that male writers don't have to suffer these kinds of diminishing labels. Just to wrap up now, it's been such a pleasure thinking about these important topics around gender and public legitimacy in storytelling. Thank you, Goretti!

**About Goretti Kyomuhendo:** Goretti is the founder and director of the African Writers Trust, which promotes synergies between African writers on the continent and in the diaspora. Goretti is also a novelist and her books include *The First Daughter* (1996), *Secrets No More* (1999), which won the Uganda National Literary Award for Best Novel, *Waiting* (2007) and *Whispers from Vera* (2002, republished 2023). In 2021, Goretti chaired the AKO Caine Prize for African Writing. Goretti is a founding member of FEMRITE – Uganda Women Writers' Association and publishing house – and worked as its first director for ten years (1997–2007).

*'I'm burdened with my ideas, and they
kill me when they don't work out.'*

## IN CONVERSATION WITH:
## THABISO MAHLAPE

9 February 2022

**Joel Cabrita:** Let's start with your own story. Tell us about your journey into publishing. You grew up in Polokwane, in the north of South Africa. How did you go from there to working at Jacana Media and then ultimately founding your own publishing company?

**Thabiso Mahlape:** When I was about seven years old, there was a neighbour's kid who'd grown up in Johannesburg who spoke English, just English. He didn't know how to speak sePedi, which is our language. That was because his entire surroundings in Johannesburg were in English. There was one day when we were playing outside our kitchen. My mother was inside the kitchen, doing dishes and cooking. The kid just kept shooting this English at me. I really didn't know what the hell he was saying because I went to a township school. So I knew really basic English and I knew words like ear, nose, eyes. You hear with your ears, you smell with your nose, and you see with your eyes. He would shoot off these questions to me and I would answer, 'I don't know, I can't see or I can't hear.'

For the most part, those questions were working out until he asked me one particular question – I don't remember what it was. But I answered with one of my stock phrases. I must have given an answer that was completely off as he went silent. My mother burst out laughing from the kitchen, which then gave him permission to laugh at me. It really made me angry. I just thought to myself, I'm going to teach myself this language, because I want to understand it, you know? So I started reading. I don't come from a background of books and literature but my dad, bless his socks, he is a very religious man in how he does things. He's got a routine and he sticks to it. He reads newspapers every day.

So I started reading those and practising words. Then it got tedious because these were newspapers. It was useless adult stuff, you know, crime, politics, all of that. Then I came across those condensed *Reader's Digest* books that we used to get a long time ago. That's when I first got lost in the magic of stories. By the time I got to high school, I was reading Danielle Steel and Sidney Sheldon. I went to a Catholic school and the principal – who was a nun – confiscated so many of my books because of their risque covers. I was quite surprised when I came to university and met students who had been to private schools with libraries and access to books. They were talking about books like *Sweet Valley High* and all these fancy things. I knew nothing about them. My journey to reading was completely different to theirs.

I knew that I wanted to do something with my career that had to do with words and stories and writing. But I had very limited access to education about what those careers were and where one could go with them. I thought that all I could be was a journalist. But actually I ended up first studying engineering, as at that point Eskom (South Africa's electricity provider) were providing scholarships to put young Black girls into science and engineering. That was the start of the most miserable four years of my life. I hated it. I gave up the scholarship. My dad was livid. It ruined our relationship, we had to rebuild it for many years.

But afterwards he did send me to the University of Pretoria to study journalism. So I walk into their career centre and say, 'Hey, I want to apply for journalism.' This lady says to me, 'Oh, sorry, sweetie, there are no places left.' I must have looked so distraught that she literally stood up and started patting my back and saying, 'No, we don't have to panic.' And she says, 'Look, this course is called publishing, you can study that. And the base modules are almost similar. So you'd be able to switch to journalism next year with some credits.' And long story short, after that, I didn't want to do journalism any more. I liked the publishing. Before I studied publishing, I didn't know that you could study such a thing. I didn't even know that there were books being made in South Africa, like the ones that I enjoyed. I thought it was an international thing, that books came from overseas. I had absolutely no knowledge of this industry.

When I finished my course, that's when the reality of it hit me. I couldn't find a job for two years. I'd done an internship with Van Schaik Publishers during my final year. When my contract ended, the head of that company said to me (they were an academic publisher), 'Just looking at you, I would be doing you a disservice if I gave you a contract to stay here'. It was a nice way to say 'you don't belong here'. But it was also a reassuring thing to hear: 'you may not belong here, but you belong somewhere.'

Back when I was studying, the Publishing Association of South Africa (PASA) were running an internship programme where they were going around the country and taking students to place into companies. They sent me to Jacana Media to do an interview. But I lived in Pretoria and Jacana was in Johannesburg. And so even though the interview went well, my boss there felt she wasn't going to hire me because travelling would be a hassle for me. But the PASA people got it wrong. They told me I was in and so I arrived at Jacana when they weren't expecting me. But Bridget Impey [the founder of Jacana] just said, 'Well, she's here now, get her a chair and a desk.' And they weren't paying for me – because PASA was paying – so it wasn't skin off their nose, really. That's how I started working at Jacana as an intern for a year, then they kept me on as a marketing assistant or something, and I hated it. Too much admin, I hate admin.

Then I said, 'Look, just call me a junior publisher. It's not gonna hurt you in any way. Just let me do the submissions thing.' I was a junior publisher for two years. In those two years, I found and then co-published with a senior publisher in the company a book called *My Father, My Monster*, by Mcintosh Polela. That really set the tone for what memoirs for Black people in this country could be. That book said to the publishing industry: you've been wrong about Black readers and Black writing. At that point, there were a few hand-picked (Black) authors who were allowed in, you know, just to pepper the potato salad. You got in really by chance and by mercy, hoping for some liberal publisher when you submitted. After that, people started taking me a little bit more seriously because of how well that book did. Then I said to Jacana, 'Well, just make me a publisher. People don't respond to my emails because of my signature [i.e. as a

Black woman].' I'd then been publishing for two or three years when the conversation around Black books as an imprint of Jacana started happening. You know, I was really feeling very frustrated, because it felt like I'd hit the ceiling very quickly.

I think from Jacana's side they were trying to lessen their salary bill. But I also think they did believe that the new imprint could work at some point. So they started talking about it with me. But I was very, very nervous about it. I had started working when I was relatively older. My friends were all accomplished by that time, they had houses, they had cars. And I was very wary of giving up this one salary from Jacana that was at least allowing me the comfort to have a drink and a meal once in a while with my friends and not be that friend that needs to be covered for.

Then I had my daughter in 2014. When I came back from maternity leave, I think that's when it started sinking in that you can't be working for like a 10 per cent salary increment every year. It's not gonna work out with a child to feed. This little girl is going to be looking up to you. What legacy are you leaving for her? What are you leaving in the world? That's when I started taking the conversation [about a new imprint] seriously. Bridget [Impey] said to me, 'You know, I saw this lovely, lovely bookshop, it was called Blackbird. I thought of you and I thought that for your imprint, Blackbird would be a nice name.' Later I went out to lunch with someone, telling him that story. He started singing Nina Simone's 'Blackbird' to me. And that's when I said, 'Okay, I'm doing this, I guess.' So we launched Blackbird Books, as a joint venture between me and Jacana in 2015. I went completely off salary at the beginning of 2016.

**Joel Cabrita:** Does that mean that your relationship with Jacana ended in 2016?

**Thabiso Mahlape:** No. I wish I had known better at that time, and known more, but I knew nothing about business at that point. One thing I did anticipate was that Blackbird would grow into a big and strong brand and there was no way I was going to build it and then leave it. So the one thing I made sure I was negotiating for in the contract [with Jacana] was that if the relationship [with Jacana] ended I would take Blackbird with me. That's how the relationship worked: that Jacana Media would underwrite the cost of making the books, so they were like an engine room for Blackbird Books. All I had to do was come with the authors, come up with the ideas, come up with the execution. I'd do the contracts of the authors, and I would have complete control over the creative editorial.

**Joel Cabrita:** How did Jacana see Blackboard's mission as different to the mission of Jacana? What was the purpose of the imprint and what was your unique niche?

**Thabiso Mahlape:** It was about who I had access to. When I started publishing under Jacana, I very quickly got dubbed a celebrity publisher, because I was publishing a lot of well-known people in South Africa. But the main thing that we discussed is that I would have a list that was all Black. I think in [Jacana's] head, these would be Black celebrities. I had access to them. So it made sense. But that's not how it worked out.

**Joel Cabrita:** You were instead more interested in publishing more of these emerging writers and in mentoring them?

**Thabiso Mahlape:** Yeah, because I had to think of what legacy I was leaving for my child. It just didn't feel enough to focus on celebrities. At that time, the rest of the publishing industry had just woken up to the Black celebrity memoir. But I felt like we were at risk of losing the art. You were seeing it happen on TV and radio, where influencers and people with huge followings were being hired instead of people with talent. I thought, I don't want to go that way. I do not want to prioritize someone's celebrity status over whether or not your story deserved to be told. As a result of that craze around celebrity memoirs – which I helped start and contributed to – we don't have a good memoir genre in this country.

**Jacob Anderson:** I was wondering whether, as a Black female publisher in South Africa, you feel you have a unique responsibility to publish certain types of materials? Or do you find that your identity doesn't play a role in forming a specific responsibility?

**Thabiso Mahlape:** It does. It does. It's so interesting for me to be asked this question at this particular moment in my life, with regard to how I feel about Blackbird and about publishing in this country. Your identity requires you to have certain ethical responsibilities. But you get punished for it, because everyone in the business wants to make money. Retail wants to make money. Authors want to make money. Your staff wants their salaries. The minute you're unable to turn over money in the way that sustains a business and sustains other businesses in the ecosystem, you become excluded. I have found it so [financially] unrewarding to be that person who looks at the submissions list and is concerned by just how arrogant and confident the male submissions are, compared to how apologetic and meek the female submissions. That's why we started the Blackbird Books writing residency for women in 2019 (which we haven't been able to do because of the pandemic). Looking at the books being published in the country, Black writers are still in the lesser margin of published books, even less so our Black women. So it's not something you can overlook. I don't think that I'd be thinking like this if I were a white man. I know Colleen Higgs does think like that, but it's rare for a white woman like her to be concerned with the lack of representation of Black women in literature.

**Jacob Anderson:** Something that Colleen spent a lot of time discussing was the unique challenges that publishers are facing now as a result of Covid, specifically financial challenges. I was wondering if you've encountered similar challenges and how you've dealt with them.

**Thabiso Mahlape:** I had a distributor, but the distributor takes 25 per cent of your revenue. And I thought, well, how hard can it be to be your own distributor. So I registered my own distribution company on top of Blackbird Books. What I had not anticipated was how the minute it was a distributor that had a Black name, owned by me, a Black woman, how that company would be excluded compared to when I was with Jacana and our Blackbird books were distributed by a big, white-owned company (or even when I was independent, we were still distributed by another white-owned company). Now my emails go unanswered. When my staff calls, the minute they say Blackbird Books, it's like they get snapped at, 'hurry, hurry along'. It's been heart-breaking to have something that made so much sense in your head fall apart in front of you.

The only way I can see staying on in publishing is to stand up and say I'm not selling to certain larger retailers any more. Particularly those with the biggest market share who sell their books on SOR [Sale or Return]. When I went independent, I said to them, 'Look, I don't think that you ought to be painting me and Colleen [Higgs, founder of Modjaji] with the same brush that you paint Jonathan Ball or Pan Macmillan. I think the discounts that you take from us should be less.' The woman I was talking to was very receptive to it. Then I guess she must have gone to have a meeting with the rest of the executives where they shut this idea down.

I have been to a party with the retailer and their CEO and he's gone round speaking to all the heads of all the other publishing houses present at the party. And he went right past me. They even created a podcast featuring the big publishing houses in South Africa. They would feature the authors of those publishing houses on the podcast, so the market would get to hear from them. And this podcast was discussed and decided upon at a dinner party at the house of the CEO. Do I get an invitation to that dinner party? Do you see how it's really just more of the same and it's so exhausting. In comparison the independent bookstores are beautiful to deal with. They pay you almost immediately. They almost never return the books, it's such a joy. But it is the larger retailers we sell to in advance before we print. They order these books and then we print numbers that accommodate those orders. And then we have them returned. I've got about R1.5 million worth of stock sitting in the warehouse at the moment. And yet to be scrambling month to month to make salaries. Our cash is sitting on the floor.

So I ended up following a business model dictated by retailers and it's not benefiting me. But because of their scale and reach, all authors want to be seen at these retail outlets. So I don't know whether we could stop doing business with them and have people still publish with us. This is the thing I hate. People push these sexy ideological bandwagons on social media about supporting Black people. But they actually don't. They're not prepared to do the hard work of standing up against certain systems.

**Joel Cabrita:** I can think of two reasons why publishing in South Africa in particular is so hard. One, it has a fairly developed publishing industry. So there are very big publishers who dominate like Jonathan Ball and so on. Then there's the institutional racism that you've been talking about so eloquently, that makes it's so difficult for an independent Black publisher to break through.

**Thabiso Mahlape:** It's really, really difficult. It's an all-white boys' club. One can't penetrate it. Each time I say that what we need for change is for all people to die in this industry, I'm looked at like I'm crazy. But it's going to take them dying for us to have a shot. You deal with authors who see people being published by Pan Macmillan having bigger launch roll-outs, or whatever, and they want the same. And I have to remind them all the time that Pan Macmillan rejected you. So you are now coming to shit on the head of the very person who's giving you a chance? I tell them, look, we punch above our weight, we really do. The business is running out of my house at the moment. When Covid hit, it just didn't seem wise to keep office space, because we didn't know how long that thing was gonna last.

And so thank God I didn't. Because just looking at the costs now, it's not something that we would have been able to afford. So that's the first problem, systemic exclusion. And then it's the fact that it's a very small pie that we are all fighting for. We don't have a big readership in South Africa, we don't have a big reading culture, we don't have a big book-buying culture, even within groups for whom money's not a problem. Our people drink champagne like you would not believe. But there just isn't a book-buying culture or a book-reading culture. It goes back to the quality of education and what Apartheid did to us. I was lucky to come to reading in the way that I did, but not everyone got that.

The other problem is that our books are very expensive. They have to be because we've got such a huge VAT [sales tax] on books and because we print very small runs, so we are unable to get lower print prices. And our printing is very expensive, which means then that prices or selling prices are very high, but also very exclusionary as is how the ecosystem is laid out, in the sense of where you can purchase books. You can only purchase books in the big towns or urban areas. There are no books in the townships. There are no bookshops in the townships where the majority of Black people live. Also people who don't have food. You're asking people to choose. There's this fantastic book that I published called *Last Star* which was the story of a taxi driver who was getting up to all sorts of things. I thought, 'Oh my gosh, people are going to be so excited to find themselves in this book.' But what I did not anticipate was that taxi drivers have to park their taxis to go into the malls to get into a bookshop – which is not what they do. So the taxi drivers drive to the malls and past the malls every single day, twenty times a day. But they do not know what the inside of the mall looks like.

There's now a girl who self-publishes her books, Dudusani Dube. She has love stories and sex, and she was able to sell. It was a phenomenon. The story just blew up on Facebook. So it's been turned into a TV series – *The Wife* – which completely butchered the story from its original state, but on TV, it's doing phenomenally. The ratings are through the roof. So it would seem people still prefer TV. People would rather unwind with the TV with a bottle of beer, than read and or go buy books. Even with people who are educated. I'd be sitting with a group of girls, some are doctors or lawyers or whatever. And they ask me how the business is doing, and I say it's not going well at all. Honestly, why? And I'm like, 'When was the last time you bought a book, any book, not mine. But any book.' And they can hardly ever answer me. Yeah, it's just not a reading culture. I was telling my best friend towards the end of last year, I said, 'Look, my friend, I'm done. I'm shutting this down.'

Another problem is when you publish Black stories in a Black continent. Ideally, you should be able to distribute in that continent. But you can't. No one is invested in establishing those distribution channels. You understand why with the big guys. Your Pan Macmillans, they've got solid markets, they don't need the African market. And you know, the little [publication] that is African in your guys' part of the world [the USA], they already own it anyway, and they've got enough of Africa. I hate this hustling mentality of one day you're doing this, and then the other half doing that, but things that don't mix. We need systems. It's one thing to say no, we're going to dismantle the white distribution system. But you've got to have a system in place yourself. Everything that's been come up with so far is makeshift, it's all temporary solutions.

**Joel Cabrita:** What about Blackbird's relationship with other publishers on the continent. Do you distribute to other countries? Do you ever have co-publishing relationships with publishers in other parts of the continent? How do you kind of situate yourself not only as a South African publisher, but as an African publisher?

**Thabiso Mahlape:** The biggest publishing happening in the continent is in South Africa. It's [also] in Nigeria, then Kenya, and then one or two of the Francophone countries. East and West [African countries] don't rate as SADC [Southern African Development Community] people. So they'd sooner go North than come here. That's interesting. So we all meet at festivals, we meet at book fairs and it's all nice and we'll hang out to drink. But when it comes to co-publications, that's what they don't like. Because co-publications mean you're still working for that money. They don't want that. What they want is to sell rights. So when I come to an African publisher and say, 'Let's do this deal together, give me your books, let me put them here, let's sell, let me send you back some of the money when we get sales,' that's not what they want. They want advances. And the advances market lives and exists only in the North.

**Joel Cabrita:** What's the power dynamic between you as a South African publisher and publishers in the Global North, in the US and Europe? Do you have any dealings with them?

**Thabiso Mahlape:** Since I left Jacana, we've sold one book, *The Eternal Audience of One* [by Remy Ngamije] to Scout Press at Simon and Schuster. [Global North] publishers do inquire and we send out a lot of books and emails. And we almost never hear back or when we do hear back, their response is that it's too South African and too African. This is what annoys me; Global North publishers almost always want a book that has migration in it. But it must be migration from South to North, or someone who was born in the North, and now they're going on to find their humble beginnings [in the South]. That's the genre they sell. We have stories with migration. It's just not the migration they want. These are inter-African migration stories. And they want a 'Jimmy comes to the North' story. It's formulaic. I find the writing that comes out of all these MFA writers, African writers on that side [in the Global North] is the same. I started reading *His Only Wife* [by Peace Adzo Medie] today. I was so annoyed because it starts off with a west African father dying and then the extended family steals everything. How many [stories like this] have we read? They [Global North publishers] have got a formula that works for them and they stick to it.

**Joel Cabrita:** All the publishers we're interviewing for this collection are women. Is this a female moment in publishing in the continent?

**Thabiso Mahlape:** I don't think it's a moment. I think it's the same kind of patriarchal system at work, where the men are all sitting in the boardroom discussing the money, but it's the women who are chasing the stories and the women who are nurturing authors, and the women nurturing the industry. When I went to Frankfurt [Book Fair] in 2019, it was my first time there and I was so shocked at how many men were there. I said to someone, 'Now, I know for sure that there is money in publishing, because otherwise they [men] wouldn't be here.'

We women are the ones willing to put in the work even when there is no money. That could be a suicidal thing we have as women, just like a burden that you are prepared to carry. But we are the ones prepared to slug it out even when it's really difficult. Yeah, I don't think it's a moment.

There are some female role models, though. If you look at how long Bibi [Bakare-Yusuf] has been doing this. Bibi is my north star. For me, her work is an inspiration. When I had the big blowout with that first book, she reached out to me. I felt so special because I've been admiring her from afar. She reached out to me and said, 'Look, it's going to pass and you're going to be okay.' And she really believes in that, she really believes in reaching out and holding people's hands. And then there is Bodour Al Qasimi who is now the [first woman] president of the International Publishing Association. And she is one person who's really very encouraging to watch because she's trying to fight for women in publishing. She does a lot of work with Africans. She does a lot of work with African publishing and supports through a foundation called Dubai Cares, which she's got huge influence in. It's just not just fleeting 5,000 rands grants.

**Joel Cabrita:** At the very beginning of the conversation, you mentioned that your dad wasn't pleased that you were switching from engineering to publishing. I wondered about your sense of professional accomplishment as a woman in publishing – do you feel you have a kind of pressure from your family and friends to be doing something else? Is your environment supportive of your ambitions and your work?

**Thabiso Mahlape:** Everyone around me is so proud of what

I've been able to do with Blackbird, which makes it all the more heart-breaking for them to watch it not sustain me in the way it ought to. For my dad, that's probably the biggest heartbreak. He doesn't say it with shame. Sometimes when he's had a bit to drink, he'll say things like, 'I wish I could buy you a house.' So I get the sense that he's worried about my safety and security. But he's actually very proud of me. He's not a man of many words. He doesn't say these things to me, I have to find out from other people. I'd be at a gathering and someone would say, 'Oh, are you the one they said was the best African publisher for whatnot?' And that's how I know he's sharing these things with others. I know he's very proud of me. But he's also very worried about what this business means for me.

**Joel Cabrita:** It sounds like an incredibly hard path to be on with so many challenges and very little support.

**Thabiso Mahlape:** Now I have to go back into writing to be able to earn extra money. I used to do a lot of column work. But I find that everyone is writing a column these days. I had a weekly staple at *The Sowetan*, one of our biggest daily newspapers. I wrote for them for five or six years. I would also contribute to other papers when I had the urge, or they were commissioning me to write about something topical. But I'm burdened with my ideas, and they kill me when they don't work out. What I really want to do is to start my own blog, where I can write about the things I want to write about. Being a fat Black woman, motherhood. I'm obsessed with how being obese and pregnant is something that's not spoken about enough. In this country a lot of obese people are actually poor Black women in townships and rural areas. I think about the medical interventions it took for me and my baby to be okay. And I worry about them. So I want to write about things like that. Hopefully, I'll be able to generate some income from the blog. That's a long-term goal for me.

**About Thabiso Mahlape:** Thabiso is the founder and director of Blackbird Books, a publishing house she founded in Johannesburg in 2015. Her goal was to amplify Black voices in South African publishing. In 2022, the African literary magazine *Brittle Paper* named Blackbird their Publishing House of the Year. Blackbird's notable books include Panashe Chigumadzi, *Sweet Medicine* (2015) and Remy Ngamije, *The Eternal Audience of One* (2019). Previously Thabiso worked for Jacana Media. At the time of publication Thabiso is at a place where she is taking a break from publishing and working for a literacy NGO.

## AFTERWORD
## KADIJA GEORGE SESAY

There is something magical about holding a book in your hand. It is even more special if you have been involved in its production. For the author, the magic is in the realization that their hard work is finally made tangible and branded with their name for others to share. For the publisher, seeing the final product is equally satisfying, particularly when the relationship with their author is a mutually productive one. Of course, the hope and plans for both author and publisher are that the book will be a financial success but initially it is not about that. Yet what is often unknown and unconsidered is the publisher's own story. This is what this series of interviews has shed light on. The interviewees offer some clarity as to why publishers do what they do.

Although, as Bibi Bakare-Yusuf states, at the same time as the magic, there is also the madness – the reality of establishing your publishing dream has to be counter-balanced with the reality of who controls the magic. Publishers often start with a passionate cause, not necessarily knowing what the endgame will be. Yet Bakare-Yusuf brings us down to earth when she relates the situation to the historic balance of power, particularly that which has been taken away from people of African descent. Bakare-Yusuf's comments regarding colonial beginnings need solemn consideration and should be kept at the forefront of our discussions on publishing in Africa[1] because colonialism retains and effects a negative impact on our endeavours to thrive. Thabiso Mahlape relates her first-hand experience of this, when the CEO of South Africa's largest bookstore chain ignored her at a book publisher social event and excluded her company from a podcast featuring white South African publishers.

Added to the historical and economic considerations is something intangible that operates alongside the physical object. This is the cultural umbilical cord which John Henrik Clarke in *Pan Africanism: A Brief History of An Idea In the African World* (Presence Africaine, 1988) explains is that which connects Africans across time and space, generations and continents. We see this when we look at the work of the generations of publishers and the spaces that they operated from. In the same way that we share historical trauma, we share historical memory.

We need to be properly informed of our history to understand the context of where we find ourselves in the present. The well-known quote attributed to no fewer than three African writers, Ivan van Sertima, James Baldwin and Maya Angelou – 'You can't understand where you're going until you understand

---

[1]  I am referring to different countries on the African continent when I use 'Africa' generically.

where you've been' – is pertinent here. I believe that our advances in publishing will be more productive once we have undertaken thorough research regarding what has taken place before and what we can learn from it. Bakare-Yusuf's historical and political positioning significantly moves us on in this regard. Colonialism rendered Black Africans insignificant and educated a select number of African people only to the extent to which it assisted them to oppress their own people through divide and rule tactics.

These interviews share a vibe that is stimulating and inspiring – the stories behind the stories. Reading these interviews, and the ways in which publishers have established relationships with some of their authors, leads me to recall the extraordinary partnership between the late Jessica Huntley, publisher of Bogle-L'Ouverture Publications, and the first author she published in 1969, Walter Rodney, and the difference that this made in the life and legacy of the publishing company. The ethos shared between Huntley and Rodney was underwritten by their mission statement; their beliefs not only in publishing but in Black ownership helped to create a model for others to use. Bogle-L'Ouverture Publications based their strategy on asking writers to contribute royalties from their first book to the publishing company to enable them to publish future authors.

Colleen Higgs mentions collegiality too, although thinking specifically of the networks between publishers. These amiable relationships are evident throughout all the interviews as the profiled women talk of conversations and advice shared. At least two of the publishers spoke of how they consulted Ellah Wakatama who advised them not to follow the not-for-profit structure. Assumptions are often made that anything of worth in Africa needs to be supported by grants and funds from the Global North. Yet these interviews show that women will struggle to contribute their own money and undertake other jobs to support, fund and keep their publishing companies operational.

However, despite many commonalities, the interviews convey that it is not easy, particularly with independent publishers, to group them under a single category. It is perhaps easier to link them through similar objectives and shared ways of working. What I will reflect on are the most pertinent issues raised by the publishers that the publishing industry in Africa will continue to grapple with in the near future. In the long term, these issues need to be considered with regard to enforcing publishing policy changes within individual countries and the continent as a whole.

The two common challenges named by all nine interviewees – that can be identified as the issues which have the most impact on their companies – are distribution and language.

Physical distribution of books and magazines is a challenge globally, particularly for small and independent publishers. Zukiswa Wanner's creation, Book Fam Africa, is a simple yet brilliant communication network between publishers, booksellers and translators to obtain each other's books quickly at a discounted rate. Expecting governments to arrange effective infrastructure for distribution, I do not believe is likely to happen. It is not a priority for governments. As publishers have already started to work on solutions themselves, they can probably do a better job with less bureaucracy and in a more functional manner. The Africa Poetry Book Fund[2] is

---

[2]   https://global.unl.edu/project-earns-funding-study-book-distribu-tion-africa.

undertaking a major research project, speaking to stakeholders throughout the publishing industry in the hope of drawing together some solutions to this complex distribution challenge. Where governments could offer effective assistance is to remove tax on books at all points of sale (from print to bookseller). Owning books is not a luxury, reading is not a luxury; it is a necessity. Anything to do with reading and learning should be heavily discounted or provided free. A literate population is essential to the prosperity of the individual and the nation.

When the issue of African language is brought into the equation of publishing, the name which most arises is that of 'language warrior' Ngũgĩ wa Thiong'o. Whatever notions and beliefs that publishers included here have on language, they are reflected in the ethos of their publishing company, helping to define it.

In her interview in this volume, Ainehi Edoro says that anything she writes about Ngũgĩ in *Brittle Paper* attracts the most traffic from readers. All the publishers interviewed have a different position on what African language provision means to them although Ngũgĩ's name is the one that most often provokes their thoughts, considerations and procedures. He is revered by all of them, whether they agree with his philosophy on language or not. Considerations range from using African languages to subvert borders practically and linguistically, translation into local African languages (Wanner), the preservation of African languages reflecting the preservation of our personal identities (Wakatama), and putting economics and investment principles first (Edoro). Both Edoro and Bakare-Yusuf discuss a parallel aspect of Ngũgĩ's philosophy linked to language and colonialism when they speak of placing Africa at the centre (see *Ngũgĩ's Moving the Centre: The Struggle for Cultural Freedom*) to enable us to move towards a stronger positioning.

## THE FUTURE OF AFRICAN PUBLISHING

The future of African publishing is Pan-African. All the publishers interviewed here have a Pan-African outlook and approach. This can be noted even in the name of Louise Umutoni's press, Huza Press, which in Kinyarwanda means 'bringing together'.

By their very existence, all of the publishers here represent Africa's future and alongside other publishers potentially reflect our common global future.

One of the pressing issues regarding the future of publishing is archiving. This is a topic that Edoro initiates, highlighting the importance of linking our past to our future. Questions that arise for me are: in what ways do we preserve and prevent the loss of material? How do we decide what is worth archiving? How do we archive? We need to take archiving more seriously than we do.

Work can be lost when books are no longer in print or when digital files aren't properly backed up. Independent presses can fulfil an important mission here. A small independent publisher may publish a backlist title that a mainstream publisher does not want to reprint, as the independent company recognizes the value of the title for their readers. For instance, Margaret Busby – under her co-owned company, Allison and Busby – published out-of-print titles authored by CLR James. With the fast changeover of technology and tools, when moving from desktop publishing to digital, much material has been lost. In my recent interviews with Black magazine publishers in the UK, I discovered that some of them discarded content that was stored on floppy disks as they no longer had the machines to access the content nor space on which to continue storing them. Magazines are usually considered ephemera, with the physical object not expected to have a long life and often destroyed once distribution has ended. This is a loss of publishing history, and depending on what was on the disks, cultural history too.

We also must find better ways for the public to be informed about archives and how they can be accessed. Social media may be part of the answer but is not the only or necessarily the best one. Not everyone uses and accesses all social media platforms. In African countries, Facebook/Meta is still favoured. In July 2023, Facebook was accessed by 80.42% of social media users on the continent as compared to 5.2% on X[3] (formerly Twitter). This shows that *Brittle Paper's* archiving of Shailja Patel's Twitter thread – discussed in her interview in the preceding pages – is one essential way of archiving such content, especially when so few people knew that it existed in the first place. At one and the same time, *Brittle Paper's* digital platform produces and archives cultural and social history, but digital should not be exclusively relied on – we do not own or control the internet space and deliberate deletions and accidents do happen. The future of African publishing should be marked by egalitarian access.

As Busby states in her foreword to this volume, the women interviewed here show that they can be author and publisher at the same time, as were a generation of earlier African women writers such as the late Buchi Emecheta. Busby published Emecheta's books originally, then Emecheta established a

---

[3]  https://gs.statcounter.com/social-media-stats/all/africa.

company, Ogwugwu Afor, to publish her own titles in hardback. A community of women writers/publishers is probably best exemplified by FEMRITE, the Ugandan Women Writers' Association. The story of how FEMRITE works together with writers and publishers across the continent and diaspora is, as told by Goretti Kyomuhendo, inspiring. Yet being both a writer and publisher has commonly been referred to as self-publishing within the British publishing industry and treated with disdain. The unspoken etiquette was to maintain distinct roles within publishing houses outside of their haloed circle. It appeared as though divide-and-rule tactics kept people in their positions to maintain a middle-class status, one in which publishers did not recognize those who existed outside their criteria – which they created to facilitate their maintenance of power and control. While the word 'publisher' has historically been used to keep gates closed, we as activists have kicked these gates open as we operate outside a straitjacketed, sanctified role. It is the acts of publishing that are powerful that are used to fight back and enforce change for good.

For Wanner, for example, publishing is about the range of different ways in which people read. All formats, all platforms. Yet there is still a discussion to be had regarding e-books which from one perspective offers reductions in costs alongside reduced environmental damage although there are also counter issues regarding environmental concerns. We should remember too that not everyone in Africa has the space or data on their smartphones to access books online. E-books remain an additional – rather than a sole – reading resource. Possibly the biggest challenge is to combat the psychological notion that African people do not read and that children do not read. If we publish literature in the way that people want to use it, then people will read it.

Challenging these notions means that publishing in Africa becomes a revolutionary act. It also challenges the status quo of what a publisher is and does. The word 'publisher' is itself an odd one: a misnomer, referring to an individual, a company or a computer application. Yet it is a word that carries power, as it is used to create exclusivity, whereas 'literary activist' is a term that should be widely embraced as it is more inclusive and appropriate to our roles and the work that we do. 'Literary activist' is non-specific yet broadly includes everything within the multiple fields characterized by literature. The women in conversation here are continually filling in the gaps to enhance the experience of readers and writers. Each of them has received at least one award or accolade for their activism.

Lola Shoneyin compares book publishing to the music business in what it can achieve: 'You can attend a party and have a fantastic time in Nigeria without playing a single track by a non-African musician.' This is more than 'showcasing'. It is akin to attending a literary festival without a single book by a non-African writer. Bringing together this collection of conversations does the vital work in drawing attention to the potential of our festivals commanding discussions on African-owned, African-directed platforms. To consider how to better support each other when taking the stage, I refer back to the methods of our pioneering publishers to see what we can learn from them, which includes figures such as Busby and Huntley. As Bakare-Yusuf puts it, 'How can we identify and proffer long-standing solutions to the damage colonialism has brought, if we don't know each other's stories, or have access to the ideas that inform our thinking?'

The strength of women in our African future is evident from

this book. They not only make the books, but they also meet the challenges of how to get these books out to readers for enjoyment and for learning. Although I attended Shoneyin's book launch for *The Secret Lives of Baba Segi's Wives* launched in London in 2010, I was unaware that she wrote her debut novel while raising four children in Britain, as well as being in full-time education and full-time work, but on reflection, I am not surprised that she did so.

There are other female African literary activists who illuminate this definition, too. Such women include Sandra Tamale, a multilingual translator in Mozambique, Muthoni Garland, co-founder of Storymoja Publishers in Kenya, and vangile gantsho in South Africa who uses poetry for healing. They have received awards as much for their innovative achievements which encourage the reading, writing and developing of writers, as for their production of books. UK-based Sierra Leonean activist, educator and author Nadia Maddy has provided a crucial resource in *The Ultimate Guide to Publishing in Africa* as a free e-directory of African publishers. Women continue to achieve in this field in extraordinary ways outside of their immediate organizations. We are authors, festival founders and directors, editors, trainers, mentors, researchers, translators, journalists, academics and agents. We are human rights activists, literacy and literary warriors, and high achievers in whatever we do to ensure we attain our goals.

**About Kadija George Sesay:** Kadija is a Sierra Leonean/ British scholar and literary activist and writer. She is the Publications Manager for Inscribe/Peepal Tree Press, where she commissions anthologies, such as *Glimpse* – a Black British speculative fiction anthology. She is also the Founder/Publisher of SABLE LitMag, the Founder/Director of the International Black Speculative Writing Festival, and Co-founder/Director of the Mboka Festival of Arts, Culture and Sport. She is developing AfriPoeTree, an app for poets. Her PhD thesis on Black publishers and Pan-Africanism will be published by Africa World Press. Kadija holds an honorary fellowship from Goldsmiths University and an honorary fellowship from the Royal Society of Literature.

# NOTES ON THE EDITORS

**Olayinka Adekola** is a computer science major at Stanford University. They love building computer systems and playing extreme water sports and video games. They were interested in working with this project because it helped shine light on an aspect of African literature that they didn't previously know about. They hope that other people can learn and take something away as well.

**Jacob Anderson** is an undergraduate student at Stanford majoring in International Relations. Having been home-schooled in Seattle before attending international school in Barcelona, Jacob is intrigued by the fields of diplomacy and education. After graduating, Jacob plans to live in Southeast Asia and Latin America before ultimately attending law school. In his free time, Jacob can be found fanatically supporting the Seattle Seahawks and rock climbing with his friends.

**Joel Cabrita** teaches and researches African history at Stanford University, and is the author of three books. Her most recent is a biography of a South African writer, Regina Gelana Twala, that documents her efforts to break through into a white-dominated publishing industry (*Written Out: The Silencing of Regina Gelana Twala*, Ohio University Press, 2023).

**Katlo Gasewagae:** Katlo Gasewagae is an aspiring filmmaker with a keen interest in the stories of marginalized communities. She studied Architectural Design at Stanford University where she discovered a love for the creative process and an appreciation for how the arts can be a crucible of memory and a means of coming home to oneself. An avid reader and lover of stories, she is particularly drawn to stories depicting how women and Queer people negotiate space and identity in the face of ever-present antagonistic forces. Katlo currently resides in her beloved hometown of Kanye, Botswana where she spends her days advocating for a culture of literacy and rummaging through the shelves of the local library.

**Bena Habtamu** grew up in the Seattle area and studied anthropology and African studies at Stanford. A daughter of Ethiopian refugees, her family trips to Addis Ababa have influenced a lot of her academic interests and research. This includes the study of urban youths and their encounters with waithood, entrepreneurship, the digital age, and how all of these experiences are surfaced in popular media and culture. Bena loves being with her cousins, creative writing, long car rides, and going to the movie theater.

**Brittany Linus** is a Client Solutions Planner at TikTok. Having graduated from Stanford with a BAH in African and African American Studies and a minor in Digital Humanities, Linus explored Black digital ways of being and doing to understand how cultural expressions transform digital landscapes into sanctuaries of wholeness, happiness, satisfaction and societal contention. Recently, Linus co-founded 3103 Barcroft Creative Agency to match young African professionals with experiences in marketing and creative strategy by providing small-to-medium sized enterprises (SMEs) with cost-effective digital talent. Her aim is to activate the private sector to achieve public good – empowering Africa's next generation of digital innovators to drive global economic growth.

**Barry Migott** holds a BS in Computer Science from Stanford. While at Stanford, he served as the president of the East African Stanford Student Association (EASSA). He also held the position of secretary for the Stanford African Entrepreneurship Network (SEAN) and was a member of the Student Alumni Council. Barry was recognized as a Humanities Research Intensive (HRI) fellow and undertook various research assistantship roles at the Center for Spatial and Textual Analysis (CESTA). In his free time, he is interested in exploring strategy, understanding human nature, and detecting deception and manipulation in interpersonal and intrapersonal relationships.

**Michelle Julia Ng** is a software engineer working in the SF Bay Area after studying computer science and history at Stanford University. Having dabbled in everything from supply-chain management to high fashion, their interests lie in the use of emerging technology to enhance innovation in other fields.

Most importantly, they are concerned about the impact of this innovation, and how we can best rethink value metrics to incorporate community impact into product building. You can find them trying new South-east Asian recipes in their spare time, or tinkering with wireless technologies!

**Anita Too** is a doctoral student in comparative literature from Nairobi, Kenya, studying at Stanford University. Her interests are around notions of race, ethnicity, kinship, citizenship and immigration as negotiated relationships to national belonging. Anita is also interested in digital innovation as a means of restoring social networks for dispersed Afro-diaspora communities. In her free time, Anita is learning how to code and enjoys comic books and graphic novels.

**Kyle Wang** graduated from Stanford University in 2023 with a BA in English (with Honours) and an MA in Modern Thought and Literature. Kyle's research interests include poetry, poetic form, and histories of anti-colonial struggle, and they currently work in San Francisco as a labour organizer. In their spare time, Kyle can be found reading fiction, rewatching 'Community', writing poetry, and experimenting with new recipes. Their writing appears elsewhere in the *Adroit Journal*, the *Kenyon Review*, and the *Cambridge Journal of Postcolonial Literary Inquiry*, and is forthcoming in *The Cortland Review*.

# ROLES OF THE EDITORS

**Olayinka Adekola:** Interviewed the nine publishers featured in this volume; transcribed interview with Louise Umutoni (including posing follow-up questions on WhatsApp)

**Jacob Anderson:** Compiled information about publishers' biographies; transcribed interviews with Colleen Higgs, Thabiso Mahlape, and Lola Shoneyin

**Joel Cabrita:** Interviewed the nine publishers featured in this volume; wrote introduction to the volume; led and coordinated the project, including liaising with Huza Press and fundraising for publication

**Katlo Gasewagae:** Interviewed the nine publishers featured in this volume; transcribed interview with Zukiswa Wanner

**Bena Habtamu:** Interviewed the nine publishers featured in this volume; transcribed interview with Ellah Wakatama

**Brittany Linus:** Interviewed the nine publishers featured in this volume; transcribed interview with Ainehi Edoro

**Barry Migott:** Interviewed the nine publishers featured in this volume; transcribed interview with Louise Umutoni (including posing follow-up questions on WhatsApp)

**Michelle Julia Ng:** Interviewed the nine publishers featured in this volume; transcribed interview with Bibi Bakare-Yusuf

**Anita Too:** Interviewed the nine publishers featured in this volume; transcribed interview with Zukiswa Wanner

**Kyle Wang:** Interviewed the nine publishers featured in this volume; wrote and edited book proposal for publisher (Huza Press) and for funding purposes